RHODE ISLAND'S
HAUNTED
RAMTAIL FACTORY

THOMAS D'AGOSTINO
&
ARLENE NICHOLSON

HAUNTED
America

Published by Haunted America
A Division of The History Press
Charleston, SC 29403
www.historypress.net

Copyright © 2014 by Thomas D'Agostino and Arlene Nicholson
Photography by Arlene Nicholson, except where noted.

First published 2014

Manufactured in the United States

ISBN 978.1.62619.639.1

Library of Congress CIP data applied for.

This book is dedicated to all those who hold legends of our land dear in their hearts and keep them alive through story.

CONTENTS

PREFACE

I, Thomas D'Agostino, cannot actually say why the history and haunts behind the Foster Woolen Manufactory, better known as the Ramtail Factory, have commanded my attention for decades. I was captivated by the story from the very first time I read about the suicide and subsequent haunting of the mill. Moreover, the rustic scenery of Foster, Rhode Island, and the ruins of the factory and village that are hidden among the brush and scrub oak seem to have a story that is literally dying to be told. It is a story that seems to have lost its verity over the ages. Facts were replaced with campfire tales, and before long, those who lived at the time of the death of Peleg Walker and the mill were gone, and no one was left to accurately tell the story of the factory and the haunting. Now, through research and investigating, I, with the help of my wife, Arlene, can tell some of those once-forgotten portions of the accounts of Ramtail once more. I am not sure how much will forever be lost to time, but I have tried my best to reveal the real description of the factory, its people and its haunts in a manner that may perhaps shed light on some questions that remain insufficiently answered to this day. There are many mysteries that make one wonder what really happened in May 1822. Perhaps we will never know the exact truths. The events that transpired during that period in time are long buried with those who lived and died with the now haunted Ramtail Factory.

ACKNOWLEDGEMENTS

This has been a passion of mine on and off for over twenty-two years. During the past several years, there have been a number of people who have helped me in one way or another, and I am extremely grateful. First and foremost, I must thank Donna Tucker-Mooney and Christine Hopkins. I am also in debt to everyone at the Foster Preservation Society for the immeasurable assistance, stories and pictures of Foster. Thank you to the Foster Library, Foster Town Hall, Burrillville Historical Preservation Society, Burrillville Town Hall, Carl Johnson, Kent Spotswood, Keith and Sandra Johnson, Kevin Fay, Robert Vespia, John Boitano, Tom and Susan Wood and Andrew Lake for his continuing research. Thank you to Brian Harnois, Christian White and Jason Mayoh for bringing the story back to the forefront with Rhode Island PBS. Thanks also to the Observer Publications/ *Valley Breeze* weekly newspaper; the Killingly Historical Society; R.J. Himes for his segment on Ramtail with WJAR's *Freaky Friday*; Dick Simons; the Scituate Town Hall; the Greenville Public Library; North Scituate Library; and musician, songwriter and historian Mike Carroll and his wife, Kathy. Thank you to the wonderful people of Foster and all others who wished to remain anonymous but were extremely valuable in the writing of this book.

Introduction

The moon begins to blanket the trees and ground with its soft eerie glow. Crickets, night birds and the howling of the coyotes become a symphony in the dark hours. Suddenly, the sonata takes a background to an ominous tolling of a bell. The clanging is not of this world, as it seems to permeate the air, echoing through the small village nearby. No one dares enter the foreboding woods from which the sound seems to originate. There is no need to. Those who have heard the ghostly peal before know all too well that it is the Ramtail ghost signaling his return.

On May 19, 1822, a small factory and accompanying homes were thrown into a preternatural realm when one of the factory's owners, Peleg Walker, was found dead in the mill. In the months that followed, the ghost of Walker would torment the villagers around the mill until they left for safer territory. In time, the mill closed and fell into ruin, yet Walker's ghost still roamed the very land he once owned in his mortal tenure. This is the story of one of the most intriguing places in New England. It is a multifaceted account of history, mystery, suicide, what some claim was murder and an eternal haunt that has endured long after the land has reclaimed the area the buildings once dominated.

To tell the story of how the little mill and village came to be haunted from merely the paranormal or legend aspect would completely negate all other equally important elements, such as the establishment, productive years and extinction of the enterprise.

To look into the story of the Ramtail Factory from previous penned words in regard to the legend by itself seems rather trite. Almost all articles ever written on the factory focus on the haunt alone and not the history and people who were responsible for its creation. When one tries to think back into the era of water-powered mills, the engineering, labor, materials and dreams of those who chose a location to execute their endeavors for a living become as enticing to read as the stories of the ghosts that inhabit their ruins.

In 1790, a wealthy Warwick, Rhode Island businessman by the name of William Potter moved from Warwick to Foster, Rhode Island, to try his hand at small-town entrepreneurship. The chain of events that followed over the next few decades would have a lasting impact on the history of the town of Foster.

Had it not been for William Potter's decision to move to Foster and take on the venture of starting a business, there would be nothing to say about what we now call Ramtail (the origin of the name will be explained later). His decision to create a mill and village along the banks of the Ponaganset River would have effects that would reverberate through the centuries, both in historical significance and legend.

There are many in this story who play an important role in the rise and fall of the factory and what has happened in the subsequent years after its demise. Each one is equally important to the history of the site. Peleg Walker is the main character of the story, but he is certainly not without a strong supporting cast. Even Amos Perry, superintendent of the 1885 state census, plays a small but vital role in the events that caused this little parcel of ruins to become known the world over.

Whether you are familiar with the history and haunts of the factory or have a newfound interest in the contents of this tome, you will soon develop a strong emotion for the characters involved in this book. These emotions may include pity, sadness, anger or apathy. Either way, you will be drawn into the story of what was once Foster's largest attempt at water-powered manufacturing and is now Rhode Island's official haunted site.

Please respect and obey all signs and postings pertaining to trespassing, littering and hours while visiting the sites mentioned in this book.

CHAPTER 1
THE FACTORY

Farmers came to work the factory
When the fields died
Potter's bell called them each morning
To the riverside.
—Thomas D'Agostino, from the song "Ramtail"

By the early nineteenth century, manufacturing had become a staple of many New England communities. Small towns formed along the rushing rivers and soon became major hubs for production and economic growth. Entrepreneurs began looking into the hinterlands for expansion, speculating that the inevitable growth would soon extend to these outer places. Foster, Rhode Island, was one of those places. One man set the course of action that would change the sleepy backwoods hamlet into a major player in the outer rim of the already established manufacturing communities—or so he thought. Instead, William Potter of Warwick became a catalyst in what would become one of Rhode Island's most intriguing haunts.

Squire William Potter, son of William Potter, was born about 1764. He married Mary Ellis, born on June 26, 1765, of Warwick on May 1, 1786. William and Mary came to Foster in 1790. Potter was a successful business owner, in addition to being a justice of the peace, thus earning the designation as squire. No interviews survive as to why he chose to move to what was known as "the Outlands" or West of the Seven Mile Line. The line divided Scituate from Cranston, with everything west of Cranston wilderness and, for the

Diary entry from Mary Williams explaining how the Ramtail mill was named, along with the fate of "one who cut his throat in the tall hour." *Photo courtesy of Christine Hopkins.*

most part, undeveloped. Present-day Seven Mile Road was once part of the Seven Mile Line. Foster, Glocester and Scituate are among the towns west of that line.

William Potter purchased land, along with a saw- and gristmill, from Jonathon Hopkins, the first recorded settler of the area. The area came to be known as Hopkins Mills and remains sparsely populated as of this writing. Potter ran the mills for a few years before starting a fulling mill. A map of Foster in 1799 mentions Potter's fulling mill, as well as eight gristmills, ten sawmills, two ironworks, a trip hammer shop and a forge.

In 1813, after running a small fulling mill for several years, Squire Potter decided to up the ante and build what was to become Foster's largest attempt at a water-powered mill for that period in time. Why would such a successful man attempt to make a go of it in what was basically the middle of nowhere? As Margery Matthews stated in her pamphlet *Peleg's Last Word: The Story of the Foster Woolen Manufactory*, "During this era of statewide economic expansion, the city merchants and manufacturers were reaching out to markets in the hinterlands creating the necessity for better roads."

Squire Potter decided to take on some partners to help with this venture. He chose his son Olney Ellis; his brother-in-law, Jonathan Ellis of Cranston, Rhode Island; and his sons-in-law Marvin Round and Peleg Walker. Marvin was married to Potter's daughter Lydia while Peleg Walker was married to daughter Mary. Together, they formed the Foster Woolen Manufacturing Company. On March 20, 1813, the partners purchased six acres of land from Parley Round for the sum of $125 dollars. The deed states:

A parcel of land lying and being in Foster on the East Bank of the river about a half a mile below Hopkins Mills and bound as follows. Beginning at a maple tree on the East Bank of said river where there is [sic] two or three maple trees standing near together from thence North 81

Dorr's Temporary Headquarters

The Foster Preservation Society presents the second pictorial tour of historical landmarks and scenic areas in Foster. It is our hope that readers will become better acquainted with the Town of Foster through these tours.

THE ONLY ORIGINAL ROOM in this house, Door's temporary headquarters, built around 1720, is the living room which has no cellar. All the other rooms have been added. There is one wide door off the living room which some people call the coffin door. There are three fireplaces in the house now, the one in the living room having a dutch oven and ash pit. The original plot of land included the land around the Mill Pond and the land extending in back of the house. There is a cemetery at the edge of the mill Pond; two of the names on the stones are Potter and Captain Walker. The milk shed on the property may have been used by Dorr as a temporary headquarters. This house located in Hopkins Mills, is the home of Mr. and Mrs. Merlin Szosz.   -Foster Preservation Society Photo

This home overlooks the Potter plot where William Potter, his wives and Peleg and Mary Walker are buried. The caption states, "Two of the names on the stones are Potter and Captain Walker." Thomas Dorr is credited to have used this home as temporary headquarters during his rebellion in 1842. *Photo courtesy of the Foster Preservation Society.*

One of the many gristmills that once dotted the banks of Foster's waterways. *Photo courtesy of the Foster Preservation Society.*

degrees east eleven rods to a stake and stones, thence north 13 degrees west 21 rods and four links to a white oak tree, thence north 43 degrees west 44 rods to a stake and stones, thence north 30 degrees east 8 and a half rods to the highway thus leads from Robert Hopkins to Robert Davis, thence following said road southerly thence following the river easterly to the first mentioned bound...

It would be a good time to note that the rod is a unit of measurement that consists of sixteen and a half feet. The links mentioned are from a measuring tool called a Gunter's chain. The chain measures sixty-six feet, or four rods, including handles. There are one hundred links per chain. One mile equals eighty chains, while one acre equals ten square chains. You may also consider that most of the early highways were sixty-six feet in width. City blocks, streets and other measurements found in early deeds still denote the measurement of the Gunter's chain. City blocks were three chains, while streets consisted of one chain length. It is quite obvious that many of our present-day measurements still harken back to Mr. Edmund Gunter's 1620 invention.

To say that the undertaking of such an endeavor was groundbreaking in Foster is mild. Foster was considered a declining and static town with regard to industry. Nonetheless, a business venture had been established, and

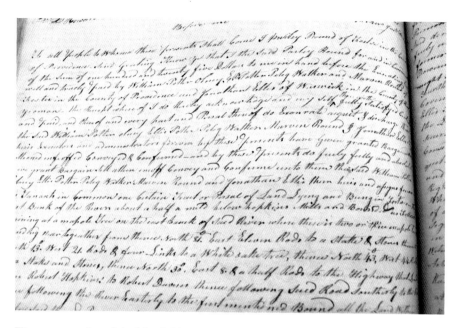

The upper portion of the March 20, 1813 land deed from Parley Round to the partners of the Foster woolen Manufacturing Company.

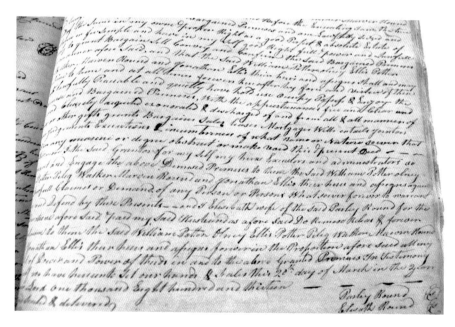

The lower portion of the March 20, 1813 land deed from Parley Round to the partners of the Foster woolen Manufacturing Company.

there was work to be done. A series of raceways and trenches was created for the diversion of water to and from the mill. It was not uncommon to have sluiceways up to three hundred yards long. In the Tarkiln section of Burrillville, Rhode Island, the remains of a sluiceway run from the old Oak Valley Mill to a waterfall and continue several hundred yards along the roadside. These remains weave past what may have once been a gristmill to another waterfall. In old photos and drawings, the man-made waterway is quite an impressive sight. The remains of the mill, now hidden among the brush and trees, still exhibit traces of the old runways where water was diverted under the mill in certain sections. The mill closed in the 1950s and was demolished for safety reasons, but the fieldstone and cement works still remain, revealing a wonderful insight in the evolution of the mill from its beginning to its razing. Arlene and I once lived on the property where the ruins sit. A neighbor, Mr. Bettis, related to us how he was hired to dismantle the massive structure, leaving only traces of history for the curious to study.

In the case of the Foster factory, a bridge to cross the dam and raceway, along with five mill homes, a general store, a waste house and a blacksmith shop, would be in keeping with the plan. Water rights had to be negotiated and secured from neighboring landowners. William Potter secured rights to remove gravel from Robert Davis's farm to fortify the dam at the cost of one dollar a year. Then there was the mill itself. It is difficult to accurately relate what the factory may have looked like, as there are no known drawings or photos to examine as of this writing. A common theme of the era would have been a stone foundation with upper floors constructed of wood. A floor for spinning and weaving, as well as one for picking and sorting and one for storage, were typical for that period in time. A garret, or attic, in the mill is mentioned in Olney's probate record as a place for storage. Then there was the wheel that ran the machines. Although it is common to depict a giant paddlewheel alongside the building, New England was subject to the same harsh winters then as it is now. This often created a problem with a factory that was to run all four seasons, as the water would freeze and the wheel itself was prone to gathering ice when not in use.

The solution to this problem would be to place the wheel inside the factory, much like the sawmill in Sturbridge Village, or to use a tub or horizontal wheel placed beneath the factory floor. The wheel sat in a tub, and as the water entered the opening, it would turn the wheel. Although this type of wheel was somewhat inefficient in comparison to other wheels, the likelihood of the mechanism freezing over in the cold months was reduced considerably by this design. By examining the ruins of the factory, it becomes evident that

The factory may have looked very similar to this unidentified mill. *Photo courtesy of the Foster Preservation Society.*

Remains of the old dam across the river from the factory ruins.

the wheel was placed below the floor. The size of the wheel pit suggests that a horizontal tub-style wheel was more than likely used. Turbine wheels were introduced later in the nineteenth century. This may have replaced the obsolete waterwheel later on—that is, of course, if the factory was still profitable at the time of the turbine wheel's inception into the industry.

Looking at the site today, it is almost impossible to visualize what the factory and homes may have looked like. Much of the stonework is buried under the soil due to erosion of the hill, the rotting of leaves and the progress of mankind over the centuries. The Hopkins family trucked gravel into the site in an attempt to raise and strengthen the small lane that runs through Ramtail. The erosion of this gravel into the foundations played a small but important role in the disappearance of some portions of the ruins. The remaining stonework gives small clues about the layout of the village. The one structure that sticks out as most identifiable is the wheel pit and raceway within the remains of the factory foundation.

The property was expanded on June 29, 1814, when the company purchased another parcel of land abutting the factory. Parley Round, Marvin's father, also owned this property, and based on the selling price of one dollar, one can assume that it was a gift in consideration of his

Remains of the wheel pit and run of the Ramtail mill.

A portion of the wall from the Foster Woolen Manufacturing Company, also known as the Ramtail Factory.

son being a partner in the enterprise. With land, the mill, houses, a store and water rights, the Foster Woolen Manufacturing Company was ready for business.

Every morning, wagons would traverse the bridge to drop off their loads of wool to be made into cloth. There are two local stories of how the colloquial term of Ramtail came to be. Margery Matthews penned in her book *Peleg's Last Word* that the name came from a process in which cloth, after being woven, would be stretched out and "napped" or loose pieces of wool clipped from the cloth. These small pieces would fall to the floor in little curls resembling a ram's tail. Another version is from a page in Mary William's diary seen at the beginning of this book. A farmer reportedly brought in ram's tails to be rolled into cloth. "Ramtail" was also a common slang word for cotton mills at the time. Whether it had something to do with the first explanation of the napping of the cloth or because it was a comical reference to the making of cloth from wool is not immediately known, but there are other instances of mills being called Ramtail throughout the early days of manufacturing in the United States. Foster had not seen an enterprise such as this to date, and although small in comparison to the larger mill towns, the factory seemed destined for success in the hinterland.

The Ponaganset River boasted several mills along its edge. Starting from the Ponaganset Reservoir in Glocester, Rhode Island, the Ponaganset River flows 12.5 miles southeast into the Scituate Reservoir. The Scituate Reservoir is a man-made basin covering 5.3 square miles with an aggregate capacity of 39 billion gallons of water. This body of water was made to supply drinking water for much of the state of Rhode Island. It began filling up on November 10, 1925, and water treatment commenced on September 30, 1926. It also happens to be the largest body of water in the state. Before the reservoir was constructed, the river converged with the Moswansicut River to form the North Branch Pawtuxet River in the area that is now flooded by the reservoir. The river itself is not exactly a raging whitewater tributary. It was, however, sufficient enough to run a fulling mill, gristmill, sawmill and, in some cases, a cotton mill.

William Potter lived in nearby Hopkins Mills, a section of Foster that began to flourish during this period. Jonathan Ellis lived in Cranston. Marvin Round lived near the Ramtail property, as did Olney E. Potter. Some records state that he lived within the bounds of the factory land, but as you have already read, the land was purchased for the purposes of a business. Olney was already settled with his wife, Orra Cole Potter, by the time they decided to make an investment into entrepreneurship. It is very likely that his land abutted the factory land, but it is not stated in any subsequent deeds. Later deeds state Widow Orra Potter's abode as being separate from the Ramtail property. Where Peleg lived remains somewhat of a mystery. His home may have been on the twenty acres he acquired in 1810. He also owned the land that the Barnet Hopkins Home (circa 1810) sits on, abutting what is still known as the old Hugh Cole property. This is mentioned several times in documents, so it can be assumed that he and his family may have occupied that home at some point. The Cole home burned and was rebuilt from the remains, but the home next to it remains mostly as it would have been back around the early nineteenth century. It is obvious by these documents that the Walker home was quite something in comparison to many of the other abodes in the area.

In regard to the daily dealings of the factory, little has been documented to use as a model for the first few years. One comparative record that actually reflects the factory's output comes from Peter Coleman's *The Transformation of Rhode Island, 1790–1860*, written in 1963. Chronologically speaking, the book mentions Foster as having two cotton mills in 1815 with a total of 700 spindles, compared to Warwick, Rhode Island's eleven mills with 15,610 spindles. In 1832, the Ramtail factory employed twenty-eight people with a total of 500 spindles, thirteen looms and a capital of $9,000. These numbers are minute compared to the larger factories of the day that employed thousands of spindles for the manufacturing of cotton with whole villages working within their massive walls.

The factory saw modest success in the first several years. After the death of Peleg Walker in 1822 (see chapter on Peleg Walker), many things began to change in regard to the factory and its partners. In 1824, Jonathan Ellis decided to sell his share in the enterprise to Olney E. Potter. The deed, dated August 9, 1824, gives Olney E. Ellis's undivided eighth share in the factory for the sum of $500. The deed also mentions a two-story home.

Deeds mention a home on the property that Orra Potter had interest in. In 1826, Marvin Round felt he no longer wished to be part of the partnership and sold his shares to Olney as well.

William Potter, now an aging man wishing to enjoy his golden years, decided to turn his investment over to his other son, William A. At this point in time, William A. and his brother Olney were the sole owners of the business. This did not last long, for on May 15 (James Arnold's "Vital Records of Rhode Island" state May 19), 1831, Olney E. Potter died suddenly. This would have not been such a crucial point in my research, but the date he died and the fact that there is no specific cause of death mentioned in the Arnold records made me wonder. Sure enough, my suspicions were founded when I checked the timeline. Olney Potter died exactly nine years to the day that Peleg Walker died. If Olney actually died on May 19, that would be the exact calendar date of nine years from the time of Peleg Walker's death. If he died on May 15, as stated on his stone, then he and Peleg both died on the third Sunday in the month of May. On both of those days, the sun rose at 4:40 a.m. and set at 7:20 p.m. It is a rather strange coincidence.

Olney's sudden death left his widow, Orra, holding his share of the interest in the factory. Two years later, in 1833, both Orra and William decided to lease the factory out to David Matthews of Foster and Darius Sherman, residing in Foster, for "cotton mill and manufacturing establishment with all buildings, machinery, and water privileges."

Matthews and Sherman paid William $1,300.00 and Orra $1,087.28 for the lease on the property. At that point, according to Olney's probate records, one more spinning frame with forty-eight spindles gave a small expansion to the mill. A clause was added in the lease that stated the lessees took the risk of water failure during the drought season. After three years, Sherman and Matthews decided not to renew the lease, reverting the responsibility of production back to Orra and William.

Olney E. Potter's stone in the Hopkins Mills Cemetery on Rams Tail Road.

Another decisive blow came to the mill in 1843 when William A. died, leaving two widows, Orra Potter and William's wife, Catherine, in full control of the establishment. In 1844, Orra, and her children decided it was time to end an era, and on June 3, 1844, their three-quarter share of the mill and all other buildings were sold to Orsumus Taft of Uxbridge, Massachusetts, for the sum of $1,125. The number of names on the deed shows that the children also had interest in the factory at that point. The names appear on the deed as follows: Orra Potter of Foster; Louise and John Remington of Scituate; Adaline and William Jones and Juliet and Matilda Potter, all of Foster; Lucy and John Levally of Warwick; and Alfred Potter of Foster. The deed also mentions a two-story home that Orra retained the rights to but does not mention why. The deeds do make mention of the sluiceway running through the property of Orra Potter.

Catherine, wife of William A., sold her quarter share later that year to Orsumus, thus giving him full ownership and control of the mill and property. By this time, the factory was still in business. Despite his experience in manufacturing, a second mortgage on the property brought financial woe to Orsumus. Perhaps he was not acclimated to the further reaches of backwoods entrepreneurship. On May 28, 1847, the mill was sold to Welcome Arnold of Oxford, Massachusetts, for the sum of $2,500. In this deed, the factory is labeled as "late belonging to the Foster Woolen Manufactory," implying that the name may have been changed when the factory changed hands.

According to Margery Matthews, production may have stopped on or before 1850. The United States census of 1850 reported the industries and goods both grown and manufactured of towns. There is no mention of a textile factory in Foster in the census. This may have been an oversight because, by 1859, Arnold had taken out two mortgages on the factory with two promissory notes held by his attorneys Shaw and Earle. Arnold moved to Northbridge, Massachusetts, and soon found that the factory was more of a curse than a commodity. Unable to pay his debts, he was forced to sell the property at public auction.

Richard Briggs purchased the factory and property, along with all the other buildings, at auction for $1,300. Briggs later sold the property for $450 at auction. John D. Cranston of Providence was the highest bidder, as reflected in the deed from July 28, 1867. It is not certain whether Cranston wished to become a mill owner or just wanted to own land in the rural section of the state. In 1873, the mill burned down to its foundation. The conflagration was blamed on local youths looking for some alleviation to their boredom. As Margery Matthews put it, "Time passed and the only visitors to the tumbling down houses and factory were fishermen and groups of youth looking for a gathering spot and diversion. It was one such group that set the deserted and derelict building on fire in 1873."

People saw the fire from Hopkins Mills, snatched their buckets and made haste to extinguish the blaze. Clara Clemence stated that one man was so excited that he tried to carry water from the river in his straw hat.

The property was sold at an estate sale in 1881 for $125 to another Providence resident, George H. Burnham. John D. Cranston was residing in

Photo of three women and a child in front of the remains of the Ramtail Factory, circa 1917. The woman on the far right is Donna Mooney's great-aunt Mary Emaline Tucker. *Photo courtesy of Christine Hopkins.*

North Kingstown when he passed away, leaving Henry Metcalf as assignee to his estate.

> *Know all men by these presents:*
> *That I Henry B. Metcalf of Pawtucket in the County of Providence and State of Rhode Island as assignee of John D. Cranston late of North Kingston in the County of Washington in the said State deceased under a deed of assignment from the said John D. Cranston to me bearing date the sixth day of February A.D. 1879 and recorded in the office of the records of deeds in the city of Providence in said State in deed book 303 at page 291.*

By the time Burnham bought the land, the factory and most of the cottages were either foundations or crumbling piles of rubble. The deed states that the factory and all its rights were to be transferred to Burnham. This may have been nothing more than transference of wording from previous deeds, like this one that said, "Also the privilege of cutting and maintaining a raceway of proper dimensions for the passage of the water from the wheel of the mill on said premises to the said river about seventy rods more or less through land late of Orra Potter and others."

This example is from Orsumus Taft's deed to Welcome Arnold. This deed also mentions keeping a "good Bridge for teams to pass." The next example is Arnold's deed to Shaw and Earle in 1849 and is mentioned thereafter in subsequent deeds ending after Burnham's deed when he sold the land to the Barden Reservoir Company. Earlier examples, in regard to the raceway, state, "through land now or late owned by Orra Potter," meaning that a portion of the raceway ran through Potter's property while she was alive.

In April 1885, Burnham sold all the rights in the lot, including the mill remains and other buildings, to the newly formed Barden Reservoir Company for one dollar. By then, the factory had already been declared haunted in the 1885 census, which means the reservoir company also purchased a resident ghost. The purpose of the reservoir was to establish a water supply for the Barden mills in the Scituate village of Ponaganset, also called Bettyville.

John Richards owned sixty stagecoaches that ran from Providence to Hartford. At one point, he purchased the tollbooth and a portion of the Ramtail property. His purchase included the land that encompassed the Ramtail property—the same that Peleg had become grantee to on May 7, 1816 (see next chapter). Clara

Wade Clemence credited Richards with razing the remaining structures when he realized they were largely uninhabitable and posed a risk of injury or death. Based on his boundary measurements, there may have sat a few structures on his property, but Burnham owned the factory and village. In May 1885, Richards sold one portion of his property to the Barden Reservoir Company. This included land at the convergence of the Ponaganset River and Dolly Cole Brook where McLaughlin's Bridge once sat. That land ended up mostly under the reservoir when the company flooded the area.

When the reservoir was sold to the Providence Water Supply Board, it became part of the Scituate Reservoir system. The Barden Company then sold several parcels of land no longer needed by it or the Providence Board. One of those parcels was the six-acre lot containing the ruins of Ramtail. Frank Hinckley bought the Ramtail property in 1927 for ten dollars. The deed to Hinckley makes mention of the blacksmith shop as a "former blacksmith shop," concluding that the building was at some time demolished by the reservoir company. There is no mention of any mill, water wheel, raceway, bridge or dam. It does mention water rights and any real estate, "including all the land, rights, privileges riparian rights, water rights, and other real estate of every kind and description, conveyed to said Barden Reservoir Company by deed from George H. Burnham dated April 6, 1885 and recorded in the records of Land Evidence in said Town of Foster in Deed Book No. 15 at pages 492 and 493."

Hinckley held on to the land for quite some time. Along the way, the Hopkinses acquired portions of land in and around the Ramtail ruins. This included the mill house ruins across the road from the factory foundations. In 1979, Martin Helfgott; his wife, Judith; Erving J. Blinkhorn Jr.; and his wife, Martha, purchased other portions of the land from the estate of Frank Hinckley for $12,000. It was around this time that gravel was removed, displacing an important piece of Foster's industrial history.

The Lucy Corporation purchased the lot in July 1984. Some locals say that it was the Lucy Corporation that removed the sand from the lot while others blame Mr. Helfgott. Either way, the owners of the land had the legal right within the town bylaws to do as they pleased with the property they purchased. There was also a tale told to Arlene and I that a certain party (name lost to antiquity) asked to borrow some sand from the acreage to fill in a washed-out road after a hurricane struck the region. Before anyone knew exactly what was being removed, half the land had been excavated. I do not know how much stock to take in any of the claims, and it really does not matter at this point. Ramtail is what it is, and whatever is left is now in good hands.

Arthur Hopkins purchased the twenty-five acres surrounding the factory land in 1900. This was the same acreage previously owned by John Richards. Subsequent purchases by the Hopkins family would eventually give them ownership of the Ramtail property. The Hopkins family preserved this portion of the acreage. Their attempts to save the site until it became a land trust recreation area in 2008 were well met and successful. As for the ghost of Peleg Walker, he still makes himself known, despite the fact that the remains of the factory and homes are now part of public domain.

> *So runs the river*
> *By the little village green*
> *So much that is lived*
> *Yet so little seen*
> *—Thomas D'Agostino*

CHAPTER 2
PELEG WALKER

People came and people went
So did Peleg's years
Hung and buried near the factory
That he held so dear
—Thomas D'Agostino, from the song "Ramtail"

The life of Peleg Walker would have been unremarkable had it not been for the chain of events that brought his name into eternal fame.

Peleg Walker was born about 1787 in Foster, Rhode Island, to William and Rhody Place Walker. The family is buried in Foster Historical Cemetery No. 54 on a knoll overlooking the Barden Reservoir along the south side of Central Pike.

Peleg married Mary "Polly" Potter on April 22, 1810. (Genealogy records label her as Polly, while the name on her gravestone states Mary. She also signed all deeds and other formal documents using Mary.) Shortly after, their first son, Albert G., was born on May 28, 1810. On September 6 of the same year, Peleg purchased twenty acres of the Walker family farm from William Walker for $400. Peleg and Mary would have three more children: Edwin, born on February 13, 1812; Paris, born on December 1, 1813; and Harriet, born on June 20, 1816. All the children would later move out of Foster and establish themselves or their families elsewhere. Albert first moved to Brooklyn, Connecticut, and then removed to Illinois, where his son, Peleg Remington Walker, would become president of the Illinois State

Foster Historical Cemetery No. 54 on Central Pike overlooking the Barden Reservoir. This is where some of Peleg Walker's family is buried. Peleg Walker is buried about a mile away.

Teacher's Association. This was Peleg Walker's grandson. As for Peleg and Mary's other children, Edwin never married, and Paris married Eliza Smith. Harriet married Charles Henry Sharpe on December 6, 1833, so as you can see, the children grew and moved on with their lives after the untimely death of their father.

As for the location of the Walker home, that remains a matter of conjecture. I have researched but cannot find any evidence left of the house. Perhaps it was demolished to make way for the Barden Reservoir, as the land the reservoir sits on was part of the Walker property. There are foundations along the edge of the reservoir on the same side of the Walker lot. The highway was there during the time the Walkers lived in the area, so more than likely their home was on the same property as the burying yard. It was very common to bury your loved ones on the property. The north side of the property was usually the spot chosen for such a lot. This was perennially the worst farming parcel of one's land due to the harsh climate that made its way down from that compass point. The burying yard is at the edge of Central Pike while the land behind it runs south. This would be the land in question. Research uncovered several documents that show the Walker family owning much of the land around and under the reservoir. By the time the land was sold to the Barden reservoir company, the Walkers no longer owned any of the property. There are deeds that mention an Edwin Walker purchasing the farm next to the Hugh and Dolly Cole property in Hopkins Mills, but that Edwin was the son of Olney Walker, the original owner of the land. That home still exists at the entrance to Old Danielson Pike in Hopkins Mills Historical District.

As mentioned previously, Walker entered into a partnership with his wife's family in 1813. It appears the business venture was going well for Peleg, as he began purchasing land around the factory and in nearby Hopkins Mills. Among his first purchases was the land adjacent to the Foster Woolen Manufacturing Company. The deed from Parley Round to Walker, dated May 7, 1816, states:

> *A certain piece of land lying in said Foster and is bound as follows viz. Beginning at the white oak tree on the east side of the highway that leads by Robert Davis at the northwest corner of said lot thence southerly bounding on the east side of said highway till it comes to land now owned by the by the Foster Woolen Mfg Co. thence southerly on said company land till it comes to the southeast corner of said company lot, thence westerly till it comes to the Punhanganset [Ponaganset] River, thence down said river till it comes to the Round Hill River, thence up said river till it comes to a large rock in said river thence north 27½ rods to a stake and stones, also the corner of Hugh Cole's land thence west 33 degrees north forty three rods to the first mentioned bound.*

The lot contained about twenty-five acres. The Hopkins Mill Cemetery was not there at the time, though there was a burying ground on the north end of the lot that was part of the purchase. Some sort of agreement was mentioned in the deed stating that the burying ground had been reserved for Stephen Cole in a deed dating back to 1808. The price for this twenty-five acre plot of land was a whopping $410.

This particular piece of land would play an important role after Peleg Walker's death. The tract, according to measurements in the deed, surrounded the factory property. Entrance and egress would be across Peleg's property. A shrewd businessman might take advantage of this situation, requiring monetary compensation in the form of some sort of toll for access of wagons through this land to the factory property. I cannot help but wonder if Peleg had considered the idea and met with extreme conflict.

The original burying ground at the northeast corner of the lot purchased by Peleg Walker on May 7, 1816. Note the fieldstone markers.

That would certainly have invited dissonance in the partnership to a point where his later dealings could become a catalyst for an aggressive solution.

Other purchases included a home and store in Hopkins Mills. The home is now known as the Oziel Hopkins home, and the store was reported by Margery Matthews to be the building across the street, commonly identified as the Old Davis Store.

Maps, records and deeds show there was another store at the corner of Ramtail Road on the same side as the Oziel Hopkins home. This would most likely be the store in question. Walker purchased this property on March 4, 1817, but sold it to Abel Hopkins in September of the same year.

A very interesting event took place in 1821 regarding Walker as a manufacturer. On August 15, he purchased a cotton mill, gristmill, sawmill, one-half of a two-story dwelling and some undeveloped land along Allum Pond, now known as Wallum Lake, in Burrillville, Rhode Island. According to the deed, Peleg had already given Harley Phillips $3,000 for the aforementioned real estate. It appears that Peleg was branching out as a mill owner. In January 1822, Olney E. Potter sold Peleg his share of the Ramtail mill for $1,000. The deed granted Peleg "one fourth part of a certain cotton factory with all my right in machinery and tools of every kind belonging to said establishment."

The Davis home in Hopkins Mills next to the former Davis store, once reported to be owned by Peleg Walker. *Photo courtesy of the Foster Preservation Society.*

The old Hopkins store in Hopkins Mills, where Ramtail villagers procured what the company store did not offer. *Photo courtesy of the Foster Preservation Society.*

According to records, the factory was moderately successful but by no means afforded the financial resources to make such purchases. It would be speculation to say that Peleg Walker was overextending his monetary abilities up until that point in time, but then he seemed to reel himself back a little when he sold half of his interest in the Burrillville venture to William A. Potter of Burrillville for $1,500 on March 8, 1822. It was sometime around this point that the firm of Walker and Potter was founded. This partnership would be short-lived. It was a little over two months later that the death of Peleg Walker occurred.

The events that took place within the final days leading up to Walker's death are lost to antiquity, but based on documents written before and after, we can piece together a good idea of what may have happened around May 19, 1822.

Somewhere between January and May 1822, Peleg's world began to fall apart. Perhaps Walker spread his finances too thin in too short a period of time, or maybe he spent money he never actually possessed. His probate records indicate that he lived well for his position. Items mentioned are mahogany tables, a horse shay, fine linens, two looking glasses and shaving apparatus (concluding that he kept his face well groomed). Also contained within are several documents with various familiar names on them, such as Hugh Cole, Samuel Saunders, William Davis and other neighbors of Peleg Walker. Other items mentioned are the eleven shares in the Scituate and Foster Turnpike Road, personal Freemason items, one share in the schoolhouse and library and a vast array of fine clothing. Peleg seemed to be living very well—perhaps above his means—which obviously spelled trouble for himself and the partnerships he was involved in. Then, in May 1822, everything came crashing down. Meanwhile, the villagers, unaware of what was transpiring around them, went about their daily routine in bliss and contentment.

The day lilies bloomed in the yards of the small homes. The small lane leading past the quaint cottages to the factory bore along its rim the beautiful colors of spring flowers. Travelers strolling by stopped, leaned down and caressed the soft petals of the sprouts while inhaling their fragrant bouquet. The tranquility that pervaded the hamlet on this day was so thick you could almost reach out and seize it like a piece of delectable fruit from the bough of a tree.

Frogs along the riverbank sang their usual arias to the morning sun. Butterflies and bees fluttered from flower to flower. The villagers tended to their gardens and relaxed in the early morning hour. The mill would sit silent

The Bartlett Hopkins home (circa 1810) was already on land Peleg Walker purchased in 1816. Peleg may have lived in this home for a short period of time. *Photo Courtesy of the Foster Preservation Society.*

today for it was Sunday, May 19, 1822, and no one worked on the Sabbath day. Everyone readied for church and shoved off up the highway toward Hopkins Mills to hear the word of the gospel. There was nothing out of the ordinary that would separate this Sunday from any other—at least, not yet.

Perhaps no one noticed that one of their own was missing—no one, except Mary Walker and her children. Her husband was nowhere to be found. What prompted a search of the mill is a matter of conjecture, but the Potters unlocked the door and entered the quiet structure. Only the sound of the river rushing by filled their ears. On the steps, there was blood that led to the body of Peleg Walker. He had slit his own throat. A diary entry from Mary Williams, who lived and worked at the mill, stated, "One cut his throat in the tall hour and it showed blood all down the stairs. I saw that look inside."

This is an interesting deviation from the legend that states he hanged himself from the bell rope, and therefore, the bell failed to summon the workers to their daily routine. May 19 fell on a Sunday, and traditionally, the Sabbath started on Saturday evening at 6:00 p.m. and lasted until Sunday evening at the same time. Some municipalities levied fines for those who dared embark on any kind of chores or work during this time frame. Religion played a major role in the administration of our society back then—so much so that towns were either annexed or disincorporated for lack of a meetinghouse within reasonable travel proximity of its residents.

Peleg was buried in the Potter family plot overlooking Hopkins Mills Pond, now Foster Historical Cemetery No. 42. His stone reads:

> *Mr.*
> *Peleg Walker*
> *died May 19th, 1822*
> *In his 35th year.*
> *Life how short*
> *Eternity how long…*

This is not a unique epitaph. There are several examples found in the churchyards of England bearing the same inscription.

At the time of his death, Peleg owed the Ramtail Factory and William Potter about $500, which was a substantial amount of money. The fact that he owed money yet possessed fine clothing and other appointments made me dig deeper into his business affairs. In 1822, before he died, he began to sell some of his holdings. It appears that he spent more than he earned, perhaps borrowing it from the Ramtail enterprise. It may have come to the point where the partners wanted their money back. Being family, it can be assumed that a deal may have been made whereby he was ousted from the partnership and relegated to something of a night watchman. There is, however, no official documentation that has come to light; only legend states that he was, in actuality, the night watchman of the facility. It is not entirely out of the question that he may have been given such a task in order to compensate the partnership for money owed, if he was indeed ousted from the partnership. This is where the accounts and the legend begin to take different turns. According to research, there are no major transactions or out-of-the-ordinary documents that gave any indication of desperation or show signs of putting affairs in order that may have signaled Peleg had been contemplating suicide. It seems that up to his death, he was going about his normal daily routine as a manufacturer and businessman. There is one out-of-the-ordinary incident that took place less than a few days before his death that made me wonder what happened from that moment until his body was discovered in the mill. A few strange deeds found in the town hall seem suspicious.

The first deed was made out to William Potter, senior partner and patriarch of the family and factory, and the second was made out to William's son

Peleg Walker's headstone in Potter Cemetery, Foster Historical Cemetery No. 42, overlooking Hopkins Mills Pond.

Olney E. The first deed, recorded on May 17, 1822, states that Peleg Walker, in consideration of $1,000 paid by William Potter, transferred "one fourth part of the Foster Woolen Manufacturing establishment with a factory thereon standing together with one quarter part of the buildings thereon standing for the bounds of said lot apply to the deed from Parley Round to said company on [illegible] in said Foster together with all the machinery and tools of every kind belonging to said establishment."

The deed also included the twenty-five acres of land that abutted the factory property and the twenty acres of land Peleg bought from William Walker in 1810.

The second deed, made out to Olney Potter in consideration of $1,000, transfers "one [two words added above but are illegible] fourth part of the late Foster Woolen Manufacturer Company estate being the same that said Co. bought of Parley Round and is the same that I the grantor bought of said Olney E. Potter [reference] being had to said deed in the Foster records together with all the machinery and tools of every kind in the said factory belonging to the estate."

I find it interesting that the word "estate" is mentioned twice in this sentence. I wonder what the motive was behind that.

I found a third deed drawn up at the same time as the other two. This deed was tucked away in another book in the town records, even though it was dated the same as the two previously mentioned. It almost seemed like this deed was surreptitiously slid into a place where it would not readily be

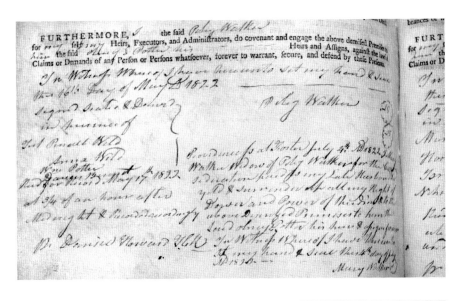

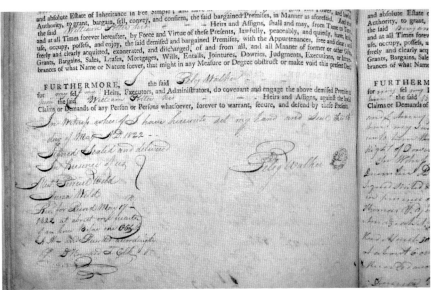

found. This deed is from William A. Potter to Olney E. Potter. Twelve acres of land was transferred in consideration of $150. This deed appears to be for twelve acres of land collectively that Peleg Walker owned but by deed sold to Joseph and John Smith on June 5, 1821, for $300. William A. Potter purchased the property from the Smiths sometime between June 5, 1821, and May 16, 1822.

The strangest detail pertaining to these deeds is that they were drawn up on May 16 before midnight and recorded into town records at 12:45 a.m., just after midnight on May 17. This would be a very awkward hour to be doing any business. Most people went to bed with the setting of the sun and rose at the first break of dawn. What created the need to write and record these deeds at such an unusual hour? The work would have been done by the dim glow of candlelight, as kerosene lamps were not introduced until 1853. Who would be in such a hurry to transfer these possessions? Another odd

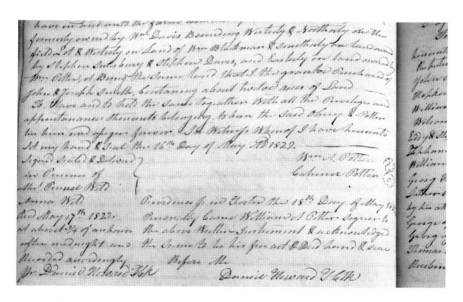

Above: A third deed drawn up the same time as the other two deeds, a few nights before Peleg's death. It was found hidden among other deeds dated much later. This is from William A. Potter to his brother Olney E.

Opposite, top: One of the suspicious deeds from Peleg Walker to Olney E. Potter transferring his shares to the factory. Note the time recorded: "¾ of an hour after midnight."

Opposite, bottom: Another of the suspicious deeds from Peleg Walker to Olney E. Potter transferring his shares to the factory. The handwriting on each was different, and Peleg's named was signed by different hands.

detail is that three different people drew up the deeds, as the handwriting on each document is completely different. The handwriting of one deed is artistic and flowing, with well-defined lines and curves. This came from someone who had taken the time to master the art of writing with a quill. Another resembles scribble and is difficult to read. Fortunately, the legal terminology contained within the deeds is basically the same, so they were easy to decipher. The script on the third is somewhere between the first two, legible but not artistic.

What also struck me as odd were the names of the witnesses in these three deeds. They were not familiar names found in the other deeds for Foster. The usual Hopkins, Potter, Davis or Howard monikers were absent. Instead, all three deeds are witnessed and signed by Samuel and Susannah Weld. A search through records finds that Susannah Weld's maiden name was Walker. She was the daughter of Ephraim and Priscilla Rawson Walker. Susannah, also known as Anna, was born in 1759; died in Providence on September 20, 1845; and is buried in Swan Point Cemetery in Providence. It appears she was a close relative of Peleg Walker. The Welds resided in Providence, which at first made me wonder if the deeds were actually drawn in the capital city and not in Foster. Speculation could create alternative endings, especially with the facts that follow within this writing. Was it a suicide? Was there some sort of argument that went wrong? Did Peleg ride out to Providence to have some deeds drawn up in haste without his wife? Previous deeds concerning Peleg's buying and selling real estate always included the presence and signature of Mary Walker. The two deeds concerning Peleg's shares in the factory and land transfer on this night did not have Mary's signature or mention of her presence within the documents. In fact, it would not be until July that we see an addendum to William Potter's deed stating that Mary agreed to the terms set forth by her deceased husband with regard to the sale of the properties. Maybe his family came to Foster to be witnesses, but why those two particular people? Daniel Howard was the Foster town clerk at the time and recorded the deeds as stated at 12:45 a.m., just after midnight. The fact that Howard was there to record the deeds would lend credence to the assumption that the deeds were written and recorded in Foster. But here is another strange fact: Daniel Howard's name is scribed by whoever wrote out each deed. Perhaps the deeds were previously drawn and Mr. Howard was there to just record the transactions. Or perhaps a more sinister motive was beginning to play out at the time, and Howard was never present. Obviously, there was a need to have these particular properties transferred right away, but by whose decision and where were they actually created?

On April 25, 1822, Olney E. sold a parcel of land he had purchased on March 2 of that year. The deed was recorded at 9:00 a.m. on May 20, just one day after Peleg was found dead. The deed was written by the same hand that recorded it. Daniel Howard was still town clerk at the time. Either Olney had a very short time of grieving for a cherished partner, brother-in-law and—hopefully—friend, or he had nothing to do with the day and hour the deed was recorded. The deed simply states, "Rec'd May 20th 1822 at about 9 o'clock am and recorded accordingly."

An interesting old wives' tale I have heard is that when someone committed suicide in the old days, he or she would be stricken from vital records, for such an act committed in these religious times tended to be a sin and disgrace to the family. I found that the Arnold Vital Records of Rhode Island state on page 207, under Walker, "Peleg, Esq., at Foster, suddenly May 19, 1822." The presence of a record showed me that maybe his death was not a suicide. Perhaps there was more to it, but again, that is just speculation. The abbreviation Esq. is short for Esquire, revealing he was a man of some stature and respect. It would be difficult and illogical to have someone of such prominence erased from public record.

After his death, there was the matter of probate and estate records. Most of his holdings were sold at auction, save for the furniture and the home. David Wilkinson of North Providence became the trustee to Peleg Walker's estate. Wilkinson is regarded as the father of the American tool. At a young age, David Wilkinson saw his first steam-powered engine. He built a model of the engine and began tinkering with ways to improve steam power. His association with William Slater, the father of the American manufacturing industry, was intimate. Wilkinson's sister Sarah married Slater, and it was Wilkinson who helped Slater build his machines. Wilkinson's mill sits next to Slater's in Pawtucket, Rhode Island, and is now part of the historic landmark.

Wilkinson was a brilliant man but not very good at business, or so history tells us. As Carl Johnson, tour guide of Slater Mill and Wilkinson admirer, put it, "He had many irons in the fire that led to his financial downfall."

David Wilkinson somehow ended up with most of Peleg's property. In fact, on June 27, 1822, Mr. Charles Tibbitts purchased Peleg's shares of the Foster Woolen Manufacturing Co. along with three acres of land at auction for $900. The deed states:

Know all men by these presence that I David Wilkinson of North Providence in the county of Providence & State of Rhode Island trustee of the creditors of the late firm of Walker and Potter and of Peleg Walker deceased for

A grinding stone is among the remains of a gristmill near Allum (Wallum) Lake in Burrillville. Peleg Walker—and later, David Wilkinson—owned the mill.

and in consideration of nine hundred dollars to me in hand paid to me by Chs. Norm Tibbitts of Providence…one undivided fourth part of a certain cotton manufacturing establishment in said Foster containing about three acres of land with factory store, dye house, dwelling houses, blacksmith shop and all other buildings standing therein.

This deed is recorded in Foster Book of Deeds Number Six, page 355. Directly after it, on page 356, Mr. Tibbitts transfers the property to Wilkinson for the same price. This transaction took place on July 6, 1822, nine days later. Wilkinson, being a trustee, was probably not allowed to directly bid on the property but could gain it later by either buying it from the highest bidder or sending someone in his place to bid on the specific properties. Either way, he ended up with land Peleg once owned: the mill and parcels of land and building in Burrillville, as well as shares in the Ramtail Factory. He later sold those shares to Olney E. Potter. The mill in Burrillville burned down about 1825.

How Wilkinson became trustee is not recorded, but he must have been a friend of Peleg. How close a friend he may have been is a course for debate.

They seemed to have many of the same personality traits, both being proud of their roles as manufacturers and purchasers of various properties. It is obvious by the historical records that Wilkinson wished to possess Walker's assets, but when he decided to acquire them and to what lengths he would have gone are now pure speculation.

Life How Short
Eternity How Long
Truer words never spoken
Nor set to song
—Thomas D'Agostino

CHAPTER 3

THE LEGEND

Legends say he rang the bell
Made his ghostly rounds
As the workers fearing his spirit
Left for hallowed ground.
—Thomas D'Agostino, from the song "Ramtail"

The tale of Peleg Walker and the Ramtail Factory is a perfect ghost story. A partnership, an argument, a self-fulfilling prophecy, a suicide, a subsequent haunting and the abandonment and ruination of the business due to a vengeful ghost. Sounds like the perfect plot for a movie or soap opera, but all these aspects play into what we now refer to as the Ramtail Factory haunt.

It is this legend I now tell that has made—to me, anyway—Ramtail Factory the greatest of New England's haunts. Of course, this is coupled with further paranormal incidents, facts and investigations of the site that have only added impetus to the legend.

As previously stated, the factory and mill village was founded in 1813. According to legend, the Potters ran the mill by day while Peleg Walker held the position of night watchman. When the quitting bell rang, the workers would end their daily routine and return to their little homes just across from the mill. It was then that Peleg, candle lantern in hand (there were no kerosene lanterns until 1853), would begin his rounds, keeping close vigil over the mill and outbuildings. When daylight peeked through the windows of the factory, Walker would finish his round by ringing the mill bell that dangled from a steeple atop the mill. The tolling of the bell roused the workers from their slumber for the start of the new workday. This was the common practice of a mill village during that time. Peleg was a proud man who fancied the title of manufacturer. He was not afraid to flaunt his position as a partner in the Foster Woolen Manufactory.

All seemed to be in perfect harmony. The workers lived in a peaceful little hamlet where their wives planted day lilies or tended to their personal gardens. The husbands spent their days at the factory turning wool into cloth, and the owners enjoyed a small but satisfying and successful business enterprise. Many of the necessities could be procured at the company store. Any other needs could be found in nearby Hopkins Mills, a short walk north of the little hamlet. There, one could attend church, purchase items at the Hopkins Mills stores or send his children to school. There seemed to be very little to worry about for the times—that is, until one event transpired that would change the fate of the factory and village forever. As with most partnerships, the issue of money became a focal point. It seems Peleg owed the factory a substantial amount of money, and an argument ensued. The other partners sided against Peleg, ousting him from the union. During the argument, it is recounted that Peleg swore to the other partners that they would one day have to retrieve the keys to the mill from the pocket of a dead man.

His associates laughed at the threat, calling it nothing more than the whimpers of an angry, desperate man. On the morning of May 19, 1822, the bell used to summon the workers failed to ring. A few bewildered employees assembled at the mill, awaiting the arrival of Squire Potter. Upon arrival, William and his son Olney noticed that the building was still locked and tightly secured. The Potters broke a window to gain access and, upon entering, encountered a ghastly spectacle. Hanging from the bell rope was thirty-five-year-old Peleg Walker with the keys to the mill dangling from his vest pocket.

Peleg was buried in the Potter plot on a knoll overlooking Hopkins Mills Pond, just north of Danielson Pike. Although the village mourned, life had to go on. The factory reopened, and the villagers' daily existence slowly returned to normal, but this normalcy was not to last.

One evening after the villagers had settled in for a good night's sleep, the mill bell began to toll. The midnight hour reigned as the ominous pealing of the mill's bell echoed through the valley. Olney Potter was immediately summoned to the mill, where he and a few other brave souls decided to cautiously enter the building. As soon as the key clicked in the lock of the heavy mill door, the tolling ceased. Convinced it was perhaps a few of the local youths playing a most unsettling prank, the Potters and a few of the workers searched the building from top to bottom but found no one inside, save for themselves. The door was once again secured, and the residents returned to their homes, satisfied that the deed must have been the work of some wily individual.

The next night, the ghostly clang again commenced at the witching hour. Once again, a thorough search of the mill turned up no signs of foul play. This time, the Potters were reluctantly forced to remove the bell rope. This did not quell the situation, for on the third night, the bell's all-too-familiar reverberation echoed over the little hamlet. Confused and desperate for peace, the Potters removed the bell itself.

Now the village, restless and apprehensive over the incidents that had come to pass, felt a trifle more relieved. This relief was short-lived, for a few nights later, the people were roused from their slumber by the sound of the factory in full operation. Every loom, spindle and other machinery within the factory started running full tilt the moment the stroke of midnight had fallen on the land. One of the villagers was able to halt the water wheel that ran the machines. All became silent, but apprehension once again ran high.

A few nights later, the same scene played out. The machinery within the building was again found running at full speed, but this time, the mill wheel was turning opposite the flow of the river. This seemed to be the last straw for the already traumatized occupants of the tiny mill village.

Workers began to leave the area for safer grounds. No one wanted to live near—let alone work at—a haunted factory. The factory began a steady decline and, within several years, ceased production altogether. Peleg's ghost was seen only once by some local folk. A few men passing by the factory late one night spied a glowing figure sauntering from one building to another with a lantern in hand. They immediately recognized the ghostly figure's gait as that of their deceased friend Peleg Walker.

In 1873, a massive fire burned the decrepit mill to its foundation. According to the legends, the blaze could be seen from Hopkins Mills. Thus was dealt the final blow to the once blissful little mill and village. The blaze may have ended the factory's tenure, but the ghost of Ramtail continued to make his presence known. To this day, the ghost of Peleg Walker continues his nightly rounds the same as he did when he inhabited his mortal frame.

On Peleg Walker's stone reads the epitaph, "Life how short. Eternity how long." If this is so, then Peleg is destined to eternally wander among the one place he loved in life and now haunts in death.

The ghostly meanderings of Peleg Walker gained much notoriety during the latter half of the nineteenth century—so much so that Amos Perry, supervisor of the 1885 Rhode Island state census, labeled the factory as an officially haunted site. If one turns to page 36 of the 1885 state census, the top line of the page includes the words: "Ramtail (haunted)."

The previous is the tale that has been told for as long as I can remember with little to no variation. There are a few changes, depending on the person telling the tale. In one instance, the bell originally pealed in the small hours of the night with an eerie, ominous resound when the weight of Peleg's lifeless body swung to and fro from the rope. Another small addition is the argument over money and the fact that he was ousted from the partnership when his position of night watchman was no longer needed. Another variation is that the factory was owned by two brothers who quarreled with the night watchman. After his suicide, the factory groaned and shook so loud it could be heard from Danielson Pike, several hundred yards north of the mill. No matter what the small variations are, the end result is the same: Ramtail is one of the most haunted sites in Rhode Island, if not beyond.

Clara Wade Clemence wrote about the Ramtail ghost for a newspaper called the *Windham County Transcript* in 1948. Here she stated, "But there had been tragedies in that little factory. A watchman named Walker cut his throat."

Lytle Hopkins one-upped that statement in his *Observer* article on October 26, 1961. He wrote:

> *At Hopkins Mills there was once a grist mill* [sic]*, a saw mill* [sic] *and a shingle mill. There was also a basket shop, a creamery and a yarn mill. The Ramtail Factory down the stream made cotton cloth.*
>
> *All of these businesses passed out of existence in a normal way presumably after having served their purpose, all except the Ramtail Factory, that is. After the night watchman was found hanging from the bell rope, dead, nothing in or around the factory was ever normal again. The RAMTAIL GHOST saw to that.*

Then there are the onslaught of ensuing articles and quips recounting the tale of the night watchman hanging himself and causing an ethereal commotion that contributes to the downfall of the factory.

For instance, in *Rhode Island: A Guide to the Smallest State*, the writer mentions the story of Ramtail on page 454. In this version, he states that a superintendent hanged himself from the bell rope, and "for years after the bell would mysteriously toll at night, and the mill windows show light."

Referring back to the diary entry mentioned in the last chapter, I must confess that something bothered me when I read it for the first time. The entry was dated 1834. Olney E. Potter died in 1831, only three years prior to that entry, yet Peleg Walker died twelve years before. The legend ranges from a night watchman hanging himself from the bell rope to someone slitting his throat. In some cases, the stories suggest that they were two separate incidences. If the legend that Walker hanged himself is true, who then, cut his own throat in the tall hour?

The story of an argument and Peleg hanging himself from the mill's bell rope has been accepted as the bona fide truth of what happened one night in May 1822. Of course, those who were alive to testify to the facts or fallacies of the legend are long silent. All except, it seems, for one who continues to roam the area, possibly looking to tell his side of the story to anyone who will listen. Arlene and I were more than ready to listen. In fact, we were ready to rewrite history if need be with regard to what may have really happened during the few months preceding Peleg's demise. Was it a suicide? Did he really hang himself from the bell rope? I had to know more, and the more I learned, it seemed, the more the mystery grew about the incidents and culmination of what we came to know as the haunted Ramtail Factory.

CHAPTER 4

MY OBSESSION WITH RAMTAIL

I came upon the ruins and declared
What vast structure once it must have been
The stones were silent yet spoke to my imagination
We were once and will someday be once again.
—*Thomas D'Agostino*

I remember my first visits to Ramtail as if they were yesterday. As I steered my van off Route 6 onto Rams Tail Road (the sign on one side actually reads Ram Tail Road, while the other reads Rams Tail Road), I felt as if I already knew the characters and scenarios that had played out over the centuries. I rolled my 1980s Ford van onto Rams Tail Road, past the cemetery and then over a small wooden bridge.

After finding a place to park along the road, I climbed out of the van, crossed the bridge and entered a field. Some fishermen had told me that there would be a path that picked up along the river, leading to the factory ruins. "One of the advantages of having a family-owned sporting goods business," I thought as I searched for the old road by the water. I spotted the road as it rose out of the sand pit that stretched out in front of me toward the woods. With each step, I felt excitement rush through my whole body, much like the feeling of that first drop on a roller coaster. I could not imagine what my eyes would behold. All I had to go by was the small article in a 1992 *Old Rhode Island* magazine regarding the legend. I knew not what I would behold beyond the first row of trees.

Left: Sign for Ram Tail Road along Route 6 East.

Below: Sign for Rams Tail Road along Route 6 West.

I walked through the small sand pit to the old lane that sprouted out of nowhere. The now overgrown dirt road that once made its way from the factory and village to Rams Tail Road had been long excavated, but there was a noticeable beginning of what was left to bring me to the place I had already dreamed of many nights before.

It was late autumn in 1992, but it felt like it could have been 1822. I walked into an imaginary world where carriages passed along the old road and villagers tended to their gardens or passed along the lane, talking of their days at the factory. The very first foundation I came across while meandering down the old overgrown trail from Rams Tail Road took my breath away. There I stood in awe over the stone remains of what was once part of the factory. I could hardly contain my excitement over the fact that I was officially in Ramtail. The wheel pit and race sat conspicuously beside the Ponaganset River. There was no doubt it was part of some sort of mill.

The sense of accomplishment was like none I had felt before. Here I stood in the place of legend, folklore and history, all wrapped into one small stone foundation. There had to be more. I walked down the old lane, looking for more signs of a mill village.

Across from the mill ruins was a wall that looked like it may have been a foundation to a large building at one point. There were also signs of what may have been smaller foundations, with old bricks tumbling out of the holes like solid lava from an extinct volcano. I would later find out that they were English brick (this was concluded by a historian due to their size and markings). The English, being mostly "wooded out," would bring bricks to America in the hulls of their ships. The bricks supplied ballast for the voyage. They were then traded to the Americans for logs and cut boards, which would take the place of the bricks as a means of ballast for the return voyage home. This would have to have been before or after the War of 1812. The war officially began on June 18, 1812, and ended on February 15, 1815. The factory was built between 1813 and 1814. If these were indeed imported English bricks, they may have been imported before the embargo with the British and stockpiled by some merchant before being sold to the partnership. Or possibly the homes were erected a few years later, after the factory started production and the war ended, lifting the embargo on commerce and trade with the British.

The remains of a well sat just astride the trail. Since the foundations were more than enough to hold my attention, I did not heed the day lilies at first. There are references in both Clara Wade Clemence's article and Margery Matthews's writing of the women tending to the day lilies that grew in the yards of the mill houses. After all these years, the day lilies still grow among the trees and shrubs as a testament to those who once toiled in the yards and at the mill. The area within the factory ruins is where I performed the first of several investigations.

I soon found myself completely captivated by the Ramtail Factory. I seized every spare moment as an opportunity to race out to the ruins, investigate them, poke around and search the brush for other signs of the once great factory. One afternoon, while I was teaching at a music store near our bait shop, I found myself with an hour of cancellations. I did the math, and it took about twenty minutes to get to the ruins. This would leave me with an easy twenty minutes to poke around before I had to return for my next lesson. I could easily run to the site to save time. From there, I could look around areas that I had questions about and run back out. Yes, I was that obsessed with Rhode Island's officially haunted site.

The large wall across the river from the wheel pit and race became a focus of a few trips to the ruins. Crossing the river was a small but attainable feat, for the boulders that once made up the old dam and possible bridge afforded a mostly dry trip across the watercourse. According to the old-timers of the area, the wall was part of the dam that was created to run the mill wheel. A bridge is mentioned in several deeds to the property. The bridge abutments east of the ruins are too far from the factory to have been part of the property. Conceivably, the wall may have also served as some sort of abutment for a bridge as well as the dam. The top of the wall is wide enough for a wagon to travel, even though it now abruptly ends at the river's edge.

Another curious landmark is a standing stone about three to four feet in height just to the right of the wall. This may have been a boundary marker or part of a raceway. Without actual drawings, the exact nature of these artifacts is mostly left to speculation.

Visiting this place is an awesome experience in itself, but then comes the thirst for the truth. History and other eyewitness accounts of what transpired over the years to give the site in question its reputation was not enough. I needed to know everything about Ramtail. This would be easy—or so I thought.

The Rhode Island Historical Society had already given me the census that named the site as "haunted," but there was more to be uncovered. My first thought was to find an old map. There were two that actually had the factory on them. One from 1862 simply said "Potter Factory." The four black squares sit on the east side at the convergence of the Ponaganset River and Dolly Cole Brook, just south of Hopkins Mills. This would indicate that the complex was actually where the rivers met about a quarter of a mile east of the foundations I first discovered, closer to what we now refer to as the "Old Round Farm."

This caused some debate about where the factory actually may have been. Could I have been wrong about the original location all along? If not Ramtail, what were those foundations in the ground along the river? I began scouring the area represented on both the 1862 and the 1895 maps. The convergence of both rivers was complemented by a set of old bridge abutments and a beaver dam that made crossing less of a task. The dam had conveniently created a small swamp, and the Barden Reservoir had covered a lot of what was once farmland. There was no way the factory and village could have been in this place, but I had to keep searching. My friends Bob Vespia, Kevin Fay and John Boitano often accompanied me on my visits. One such visit found us on the east side of the swamp attempting to climb

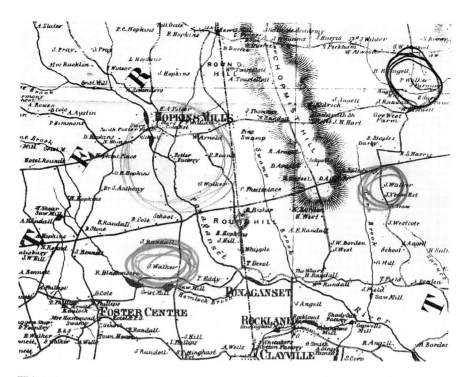

This 1862 map of Foster still shows the Ramtail village, but it is labeled "Potter Factory."
Map courtesy of the Foster Town Hall.

a steep hill. The high grass along the side of the marsh made it difficult to see past where we were standing, and several times I ended up in ankle-deep mud. The horseflies were more than happy with our presence and let us know with full vigor. I swore I would never again venture into such an area when the horseflies were out in full force. Of course, that self-proclamation was to be broken countless times over the coming years. I will not bore you with how many ticks we had to pull off ourselves or how many horsefly bites we sustained, but it became part of the normal routine of visiting Ramtail during the hot summer months.

It was the deeds that solidified the actual location of the ruins. By re-creating the boundaries marked on the deeds, I was able to once again reassure myself that the Ramtail Factory and mill home ruins were those I had first spied on my early visits. I had to take into consideration that the first map may have misrepresented the location of the village, and subsequent maps also used this misinformation.

The later map also shows the area without any markings to indicate where the buildings may have once stood. This was somewhat helpful in pinning down a timeline, but I needed more precise dates of when the factory closed and burned. Unfortunately, there were no other maps explicit enough to aid in this quest.

Foster Old Home Days is one of the last rural celebrations in the state. Every year since 1904, the town gets together and holds a real down-home fair, complete with tractor pulls, sheep shearing, baking contests, music and cow chip bingo. Yes, that's correct, cow chip bingo. I am not sure if you can bring your own cow chip, but they give prizes to the best "chippers." For those of you who are not familiar with exactly what a cow chip is, let me elaborate. A cow eats grass and digests what will later become a cow chip. Once the sun has done its job, you have a good solid cow chip. Let the games begin.

It was during one of these fairs that I came across the booklet *Peleg's Last Word: The Story of the Foster Woolen Manufactory* by Margery Matthews. Matthews was one of Foster's prominent historians. She was awarded the Rhode Island Historic Preservation Award for her work in preserving the history of the area and was the first female president of the Foster Town Council. Arlene and I were taken aback for a moment by the find, but

Foster Center, where Old Home Days has been held since 1904, has not changed much over the past one hundred years. *Photo courtesy of the Foster Preservation Society.*

before I could even take another breath, the book was paid for and in a safe and secure place in Arlene's pocketbook. Reading the pamphlet was easy, but it was the bibliography I was really interested in. I hoped to find more information on the factory, and sure enough, I did.

One of the references Ms. Matthews cited was an article from the October 26, 1973 edition of the *Observer* weekly newspaper out of Greenville, Rhode Island. I called the paper's main office and was told that the Greenville Public Library had every issue ever printed transferred to microfilm. This is sort of near and dear to my heart, as I once worked for the *Observer* while in high school. The main office was across from Greenville Avenue in Greenville, where I grew up. The library was about one hundred yards east on Route 44 from the driveway of the *Observer* office.

Once inside the library, I sat down at the antiquated microfiche machine, staring at the old knobs and switches. The reference librarian inquired, "Do you know how to use one of these?"

"Not like this," was my brief and bewildered answer.

"It is rather old," she said, "but it was donated, so we can't complain. Here, let me show you how to load the film."

After a brief tutorial on the arcane unit, I was off and reading. As I rolled through the pages, millions of images flashed in my memory, bringing back all the recollections of seeing those exact pages in my youth. Disjointed thoughts became clear as I scrolled through the issue, and then the spell was broken. I slowly centered the page, and my heart began to race. I *knew* that article. I remembered that article when it was first published. My jaw literally dropped, and I said something out loud but cannot remember what it was. I only remember some of the patrons and the librarians looking over as if I had just seen a ghost. I believe I did. It was a ghost of my past. The article not only told the tale of Ramtail but also of the ghost of Dolly Cole, another closely related haunt that I will describe in more depth later. It was this article I once read on that October day in 1973 that made me realize I had seen the ghost of Dolly Cole one year before. That was my first ghost, and let me tell you, you never forget your first ghost.

After another quick tutorial on how to make copies of the article, I eagerly began pumping out the pages. Not one but several would suffice. Much to my disappointment, the copier was even more antiquated than the microfilm reader. The librarians did not charge me for the copies, as they knew this fact. It took several adjustments to create a legible copy of the article for my records. With some manipulation of color and shading, I produced an adequate copy of the article to take home and scan on a more modern machine.

Page 36 of the 1885 Rhode Island state census clearly states that Ramtail Factory is haunted.

Next was the Lytle Hopkins 1961 *Observer* article on the Ramtail Factory. Mrs. Hopkins lived on Route 6, across from the Hopkins Mills Cemetery, the property once owned by Peleg Walker. If anyone had a story to tell, it was she. Her article narrates the story much like others before and after but in a fashion more suited for the Halloween season. After perusing Lytle Hopkins's article, I turned my attention to Amos Perry, superintendent of the 1885 census. Why did Mr. Perry make such an entry? One must admit it is quite a bold statement for such a stoic work. A brief sketch of his life will provide some answers to the previous query.

Amos Perry was born on August 12, 1812, in the village of South Natick, Massachusetts. He graduated from Harvard University in 1837. He married Elizabeth Anastasia Phetteplace of Gloucester, Massachusetts, on August 28, 1838.

In 1841, Brown University conferred upon him the degree of master of arts. Griswold College in Iowa made him a doctor of laws. He became an educator and traveled abroad between the years of 1837 and 1859. While Perry was traveling abroad in 1861 and 1862, President Abraham Lincoln appointed him as diplomatic and consular agent at the Court of His Highness, the Bey of Tunis. He was promoted to ambassador in 1865.

In 1873, he became secretary of the Rhode Island Historical Society and, by 1880, was the librarian for the society. Amos Perry died on August 10, 1899, in New London, Connecticut. It appears Mr. Perry took more to the arcane aspects of history. An entry pertaining to his census work of 1885 from the Rhode Island Historical Society Proceedings for 1899 states, "In his report may be found historical accounts of unusual value, such are not often found in census compendiums."

That is an understatement, to say the least.

CHAPTER 5

RAMTAIL OR ROUND FARM?

Lo and behold the land you see
For if there is but one place to be,
Where haunts before you flee
It is here among the twig and tree.
  —Thomas D'Agostino

A few months passed before I began to notice empty Styrofoam containers strewn about the river's edge. I knew these all too well. They were worm and night crawler cups, the remnants of fishermen who were less than respectful of what was now to me an almost sacred site. The idea of them being there would not have had such an impact on me if it were not for the fact that these containers of bait were purchased at the R&Y Shop, the same shop that my family founded in 1975.

New mission. While tending the store there (which I did very often), I would endeavor to ask where the eager sportsmen might be going fishing. I made it a point to mention the Ramtail area in hopes a store patron might have some sort of story to share in regard to the history and haunting.

It was during one of these rehearsed "spontaneous" banters that I was told by an avid visitor to the Ramtail site that the factory was actually across the river, just past the beaver dam. There was once a bridge there, but all that remains as of this writing is the abutments on each side. Beavers, eager to build a new home in a serene setting, actually dammed the river at the crossing. They are certainly crafty and worthy of their due as engineers.

Their toils made it easy to amble across the river to where my patron swore the ruins of the old factory were located.

"I go there but only in the day time now," the fisherman said.

"You mean the large foundations on the opposite side of the river from the Hopkins Mills Cemetery?" I asked.

"Yeah, that's the factory and houses. At least, that is what I grew up being told," he answered.

I pondered the possibility of those ruins being the site of the actual factory or at least a factory. He continued, "They say you can see the ghost of the night watchman who hanged himself still making his rounds. His lantern is sometimes seen at night. There's also a bell that rings out there. You know, he hung himself from the bell rope of the factory. I stay near the dam when I am alone. That kind of stuff freaks me out."

Arlene and I met Dick Simons while exploring the area around Hopkins Mills Pond. We spoke at length about the history of the factory and Peleg Walker. Dick related some really interesting perspectives on the location of the mill. Dick lives on the property across from the Ramtail area. "The cotton mill is right across the river from here," Dick said, pointing to the woods directly across from his yard.

Near the bridge abutments at the convergence of the Ponaganset River and Dolly Cole Brook, beavers built a dam, making for an easy of crossing. This convergence is what separates the two sets of ruins, both thought to be part of the Ramtail factory and village. *Photo courtesy of the Foster Preservation Society.*

"There were three mills: a gristmill, sawmill and the cotton mill. The ruins of the cotton mill are there, the sawmill was over there," he said, pointing to where the beaver dam was, "and the gristmill ruins sit where the Ramtail dam was. Peleg Walker supposedly killed himself in the sawmill."

"What about the other foundations?" I asked.

"What foundations?" he replied.

"The ones across the path from the cotton mill. There is a cellar hole of a building with a sloped entrance and another with a basement containing the remains of a fireplace. I thought that was the Round Farm," I said.

Dick chimed in, "The home with the fireplace was the mill owner's home. The Round Farm was toward Central Pike. I am not sure what the other foundation was, but there are small walled-in areas for livestock."

Now that I think of it, Orra Potter's residence is stated as being on the property in the deeds. Also mentioned is the fact that the sluiceway ran about twenty rods to the mill. That is quite a distance. The ruins Dick stated as those of the cotton mill are about that distance from the bridge

Remains of a large building, most likely a barn, at the old Round Farm. Some claim this structure to be the Ramtail Factory ruins.

The cellar hole of a home across the path from barn ruins at the Round Farm. The remains of a central fireplace in the cellar hole proves that it was the home and not an outbuilding.

remains. There is also a small foundation that was once a blacksmith shop. This is evidenced by the stonework remains of the structure found within the confines of what we call the Round Farm. This would most definitely correspond with the location of the factory as seen on the old maps of Foster. The other compelling fact that concerned me as to which site was the real factory was that several witnesses spied a ghostly light in this area. Is this the real factory, and the village was across the river where the dam ruins sit? This would mean that the small foundation by the river was actually a gristmill, and the Barden Reservoir, when created, flooded some of the mill property. Unfortunately, there are no records explicit enough to puzzle out the exact location and nature of the ruins we see today. Maybe the night watchman was in charge of looking after all three mills and therefore meandered back and forth along the small lane over the bridge and back, making sure all was secure. This would certainly account for the need for a night watchman and the ghostly lantern flame being spotted in both places.

Another regular at Ramtail had this story to relate:

One night, I and a few other friends decided to camp out at the factory ruins for opening day. When six o'clock came, we walked over to the beaver dam and threw our lines in the water. It was still dark, but we could see pretty well. Suddenly, there was this strange mist that rose from the pool where the bridge spits out. It formed what looked like a real person hovering over the water. We grabbed our gear and were outta there in no time. We left the bait we got from Rudy [my father], but there was no goin' back. You do ghost hunting. You should check out the place. You have to park on Rams Tail Road and cross the river. The ruins to the factory are up a bit, but the thing we saw was right in the middle of the pool where the bridge was.

That is why I began investigating the other ruins across the old beaver dam. And, if I may say, they hold as much mystery as the actual factory itself. It seems life in Ramtail goes on long after death—perhaps for all eternity, but we may never know that for sure.

The walk to the farm site from Rams Tail Road is not as long as from Central Pike, but there is only one obstacle: the river. Dolly Cole Brook crosses the trail leading to the ruins that I was told were the old factory. This is where the aforementioned beaver dam, when intact, made crossing an effortless task. Once across, the road leads up a small incline to ruins of several buildings. If this was the factory, it was much more dynamic from a visual standpoint than the other ruins. No matter what, the place needed to be investigated, and I was ready to do some investigating.

From the point where you would cross the stream, stone walls line the old lane, forming a well-defined road. The road leads to the first foundation on the right. In fact, the wall of this foundation is only a few feet from the trail. This is a rather large foundation with tall walls on the side of the road and a low wall in the center. The side away from the road has little, if any, sign of a wall. On the left side of the trail sit two other foundations. One had a basement with a central fireplace, and another had only the cellar hole. I figured this was some sort of small building, but the one with the remains of the fireplace in the basement was more than likely a home. These structures, along with the remains of a well, gave me the impression that it was more a farm than a mill village. Deep within the remote corner of the large foundation were the remnants of a wagon. Springs, pieces of wood and the metal rims of a wheel were found amid the brush and leaves. I was really interested in the historical aspect of the site at this point, but it was the stories and experiences that made me believe that there was more to this site than just an old farm.

With one camp believing that the farm site is Ramtail and another the mill and village site, I began to ponder the possibility that over time, the two sites became one in legend. Perhaps the ghostly lantern light is a member of the Round family, still making his nightly check of the farm that is but rubble and ruin but, in his world, still healthy and prosperous.

I honestly must say that I feel both sites compose Ramtail as a whole. Some say that the ruins on the private property side of the beaver dam are remains of the old Round Farm. They may very well be, although maps show the placement of the Round property closer to Central Pike. Perhaps they were once part of a mill or some offshoot of the Ramtail Factory and village. The land is part of the Providence Water Supply Board and therefore off-limits to the general public. It does not matter much that the land where the "farm" ruins sit is private property, for it has been established that the ruins next to the dam are that of a mill and mill homes. This may be accepted as fact, but with regard to whether the other ruins are those of the Round Farm, I say maybe Dick Simons is on to something worth looking into a little deeper.

By the ruins of an old mill
Down where the waters flow
Behold a strange figure in the night
By the light of an eerie lantern's glow.
—Thomas D'Agostino

CHAPTER 6

RAMTAIL TODAY

History made us think
Legend made us wonder
Time came and went
And the truth came out from under.
—*Thomas D'Agostino*

The cool waters of the Ponaganset flow over the boulders that once served as a dam. Hikers stroll along the old trail, their dogs wagging their tails, content to be on a walk with their humans. Fishermen toss their lines in the tributary, hoping for some sport while the rest of the local wildlife goes about its daily routine. There is a new peace that pervades the former hamlet. It is one now governed by nature.

Most of the visitors have no idea where the ruins are located or what the actual history of Ramtail is. They only feel the deep tranquility and serenity that has since cloaked the woods. Whenever I visit Ramtail, I feel the same way. It is a place to sit and relax, a place to contemplate or read among the old stonework. It is a place where, no matter what you may know about the factory and its haunting, you still feel drawn to the warmth the woods now provide during the day.

When passing by the traces of ruins that compose the last vestiges of the factory and village, it becomes hard to imagine what the area may have looked like. There are mounds and stone walls scattered about the little village, but nature has reclaimed most of the once cleared land. Even within

The old road that leads to Ramtail.

the visible remains of what was once a home or waste house stand tall maple and oak trees. A 1974 map of the area shows a few cellar hole drawings along the old road but not much else. Day lilies still sprout about the remains of what was once the small but sufficient yards of the mill cottages, and there is a small pothole that resembles a filled-in well.

I have walked almost every inch of the area in hopes of finding more that would give me some indication of a clear-cut idea pertaining to the layout of the village. I tried to imagine what the builders of the time might have taken into consideration when erecting the homes and other buildings. How were they spaced? How far from the factory would these homes have to be situated? I pondered these and other questions. I did not have to imagine for very long. During a weekend ghost hunt event we were hosting at the Eastover in Lenox, Massachusetts, one of our guests came forth and introduced herself as someone who had grown up around the Ramtail property. Her name is Donna Tucker-Mooney, and her father, Norman Tucker, was a town historian and knew a great deal about the legend. He grew up playing among the foundations and bathing in the Ramtail swimming hole. They lived across Route 6 in the Hopkins Mills District, just north of Ramtail. Norman's grandmother actually worked at the factory around the time Peleg Walker died. It is her diary entry that is reproduced in the beginning of this book. Donna was pleased about our interest in the history of the factory and promised to show us the finer points when we returned to Rhode Island. The weekend in the Berkshires was great. The Eastover was a summer estate turned resort that was—as you may have guessed—haunted.

Bob Hughes and Vickie Julian-Hughes were regulars to the Eastover. Having found out the resort tenanted some ghosts, they immediately suggested we might plan a special event for a complete weekend. The event was a special ghost hunt weekend where guests came to investigate the 1,500-acre resort. Several buildings were reputedly haunted, and no stone was left unturned. We captured some strange evidence of the haunting in the form of electronic voice phenomena (EVPs) and made some new friends. It was a memorable weekend, by all accounts. Next was the unmasking of Ramtail, once and for all.

A few weeks after our Berkshire event, Arlene and I were at Ramtail with Donna when she began showing us the remains of the homes and store. If you were not looking for the ruins, you would no longer recognize

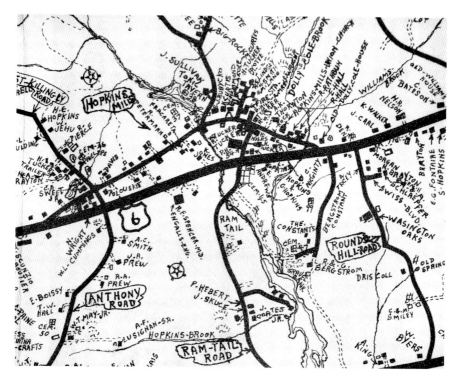

A 1974 map shows where the Ramtail ruins are located. Cellar holes and other remains are marked by broken rectangles along the Ponaganset River. *Map courtesy of the Foster Preservation Society.*

them. Donna assured us, "When we were children, the foundations were very distinct and easy to spot. We would bring the cows to the fields, which then had no trees. That's why they were called the flats. It was all hay fields then. The foundations were used as dump holes." Donna chuckled, "You see, back then there was no garbage pickup, so it was considered 'considerate' to throw your garbage in a hole. Dennis Hopkins slowly began to fill the cellar holes, and over time—maybe for safety reasons but whatever the reason—the remains of the homes and other buildings became barely visible."

Donna continued to speak as she pointed out every home and even what may have been the company store.

What you see today is not at all what we saw as kids. The bridge was still there. It was wooden planks, and we always called it McLaughlin's Bridge but no one knows why. Even the old-timers called it that, but no one named McLaughlin ever lived in the area. The gravel road led from Rams Tail Road, along the river and straight through the village. There were no trees or brush; it was not overgrown at all like it is today. We would sit on the tailgate of the pickup truck and drive down to Ramtail. There were no branches or brush to hit us as we rode in back of the truck. We would then dump our garbage in the holes. My family also charcoaled in the flats. They [Donna's uncles] would move from one spot to another while making charcoal pits for the coal.

This is true. Save for some tumbled bricks, stonework and the old refuse flowing out of the ground, the foundations of Ramtail have become almost invisible to the naked eye, except, of course, the dam, wheel pit and sluiceway that clearly confirm the location of the former mill. At one point, the buildings stretched all the way from the mill to Rams Tail Road.

Excavations of the land were of no help to the historical preservation of the area. Fortunately, the Foster Preservation Society owns a few old photos of some of the ruins that were taken just before the land was excavated. I also discovered the remains of one of the home ruins hidden among the brush and partially excavated earth. It was an important discovery because it helped to estimate the size of the mill and village as a whole. One other interesting discovery was the small gravel pit on the old Davis property that William Potter used to fortify the dam. I had discovered this many years ago and thought nothing of its presence until Andrew Lake brought the site and its former use to my attention.

Ruins of the company store in the Ramtail village.

Trees, brush and rubble are the only items left in the cellar holes of the mill homes at the village of Ramtail.

In 2008, the area of Ramtail became part of the Foster Land Trust with the goal of preserving the land for all to enjoy. The trail starts at Rams Tail Road and ends at the remains of the old bridge once used to cross the confluence of the Ponaganset River and Dolly Cole Brook. There is a small plaque on a tree to the right side of the trail, just past the factory ruins, marking the land trust boundary. For those who wish to explore the area further, there is a hiking trail around the Barden Reservoir, on the other side of Central Pike across from the private property side of Ramtail.

Since my first article on the Ramtail Factory for *FATE* magazine was published many years ago, countless articles on the site have appeared online and in newspapers, magazines, books and other publications. The site has appeared in three documentaries for cable television and Public Broadcast Systems, and people from near and far have made a pilgrimage to visit Rhode Island's official haunt. Although it seems that the small nineteenth-century village has really made it into the twenty-first century, Arlene and I strive to keep Ramtail back in the time when the water wheel turned the spindles and looms and the villagers planted day lilies in their yards. The Ramtail of yesterday is what we wish to remain for today and tomorrow, both in our minds and in our hearts.

CHAPTER 7

THE GHOSTS OF RAMTAIL

Now the ruins lit by lantern
From Peleg Walker's glow
As the spirit walks the floors
That burned down long ago.
—*Thomas D'Agostino, from the song "Ramtail"*

There are at least one hundred prologues I could write in regard to the commencement of this chapter, but they will all eventually funnel into the same ending. The tale that led to the demise and haunting of the little village has been penned as far back as the late nineteenth century. Since then, countless legend trippers have made pilgrimages to the area in search of the famous Ramtail ghost we know as Peleg Walker.

The weaving of tale, truth, fact and folklore has made this account one that transcends the romantic old-fashioned ghost stories. It is that romanticism that has captured my attention for so many years. It is that feeling you get when you hear your first scary ghost story, the one that you remember almost verbatim. It is the story you tell every opportunity you get. Even as an adult, that once-terrifying tale that kept you wide eyed and awake at every bump in the night is still held dear in your heart. I actually felt that I did not want to know more about the history and haunts of the factory because I was afraid the legend I fell in love with would be ruined, as far as the romanticism of the tale goes. In this case, the discoveries only fueled that feeling I first had when I read about the night watchman who hanged himself from the factory bell rope, keys to the mill dangling from his pocket.

The many accounts of phantom bells tolling, ghostly lanterns lighting, old lanterns creaking and glowing ethereal forms moving about the ruins of the decaying foundations are a testament to why Arlene and I have returned so many times to see or hear more.

One visit to the old Ramtail mill fills one's mind with unfinished scenes of the past and what the mill and homes may have looked like in their heyday. What were the people like, and most of all, what actually transpired on that evening in May 1822?

I wanted to know. I *needed* to know. It was as if some mystical force had chosen me to puzzle out the history behind the Ramtail Factory. What led up to the horrible account that made this otherwise obscure site a legend in the annals of Rhode Island?

As I approached the ruins for another of my countless visits, the same familiar feeling once again invaded my senses. It was beautiful, serene and almost surreal. It was hard to grasp the reality that such a tragedy had taken place on this very spot almost two hundred years ago. The bubbling brook cascaded over boulders that once served as a dam and bridge across the Ponaganset River. Remnants of a sluiceway, wheel race and bridge abutment made it hard to conceive that a mill, houses and other outbuildings once graced this parcel of land along the river. The woods had reclaimed most of the area, reigning sovereign over everything—everything, that is, but the ghost.

I have been to Ramtail at least one hundred times, if not more, and yet it still retains the magic I felt on my first visit. Even the mill houses and company store are but small piles of rubble and brick mostly hidden under leaves, soil and brush, but they still have something to tell of the history that makes Ramtail so alluring. It is this allure that keeps us going back to find more answers. Our many investigations have proven beyond a shadow of a doubt that the Ramtail Factory is still tenanted by spirits of the past. Other investigations and accounts told in this book by different parties only solidify that declaration.

My first visit to Ramtail in 1992 was not to investigate as much as it was a legend trip. In my mind, I pictured a decrepit mill, complete with a rotted or crumbling waterwheel or perhaps some sluiceway where water still trickled down grazing the remains of the old wheel. I knew the mill had burned, but I still hoped for some sort of wood to be left standing. Nonetheless, I was awestruck by the fact that I had stood in a place that was revered enough to

be called "haunted" in the 1885 state census. After my first
mentioned, I felt I was ready to go the distance with a nigh.

My first paranormal encounter at the site came shor
few treks into Ramtail. My friend John Boitano and I d
nighttime vigil at the site. Armed with a flashlight, record and our keen
sense of adventure, we embarked on what was going to be quite an evening.
John and I meandered through the small sand pit along Rams Tail Road
that led to the old overgrown lane. The road once spilled out to the main
road, which went by the name of Davis Road before it was renamed Rams
Tail Road. The small dirt road was among the history that was obliterated
when the property became a gravel pit.

Just embarking down that road always gave me a thrill much like the first
drop of a roller coaster ride. It had long been dark by the time we made our
way along the road that ran along the river's edge, but I was already well
accustomed to the area. I chose to visit at about 9:00 p.m., as that would be
about the time the villagers would have set off to bed and a night watchman
might begin his rounds. We arrived at the main foundation and set up our
vigil there. The darkness was in itself almost supernatural. To see a ghost
would be a stroke of luck for sure, but for some reason, I felt an instant
connection with the place. It was a Wednesday night, and the woods were
so dark that we could barely see our hands in front of our faces. This would
be the scenario more times than I can remember. It was then that I realized
we should have taken a few more lights, but one would have to do. Besides,
I did not want to light the place; I wanted to see the mysterious candlelight
from Peleg's lantern. Lights of our own would defy our original intentions.

So there we stood in the dark, waiting for Ramtail to come to life.
Would we see the ghost of Peleg Walker "sauntering" from ruin to ruin,
or would we hear the phantom bell toll? Perhaps we would experience
both or hear the sounds of the long-burned mill come to life with whirring
looms and spindles.

Forty-five minutes had passed when our small talk and banter was
interrupted by something that formed in front of us within the factory
ruins. At first it was a small ball of light, but it grew to a long, hazy form of
about average human height. At the same time we saw this glowing form,
there seemed to be a sudden silence in the sounds of the night. There were
no chirps, peeps or any other indication that the woods were inhabited by
anything other than ourselves and the glowing form. It barely resembled
any human shape as it floated several feet above the ground, moving slowly
from the main building ruins to what may have been the waste house before

returning to the main building. We both stood there, entranced by the apparition, which seemed completely unaware of our presence. I cannot say how long—perhaps ten seconds, perhaps thirty—before it just vanished, but whatever it was, we never actually expected to see the famous glowing light. As the form moved through the trees, it was clear that it was not being produced by anything human. This was unquestionably not from our realm. The whole time, I was trying to figure out what natural phenomena would cause such an apparition. Deep down, I knew what it really was: Peleg, or someone else, was making his rounds. The glowing mass had appeared and vanished right in front of us. The insects and other wildlife once again resounded, as if someone had turned them back on.

We did not need to stick around for a second showing.

In James Earl Clauson's book *These Plantations*, the story has Peleg hanging himself from the bell rope after the famed argument followed by the usual ghostly shenanigans. One detail that stuck out is about the men who witnessed Walker's ghost: "Three men one cold winter night, passing nearby, caught a glimpse of a figure all in white and swinging a lantern pass from the mill door to the waste house, disappear for a moment and return to the mill."

I found the book in a used bookstore located in North Kingstown, Rhode Island, about five years prior to this writing and about fifteen years after the above incident. I was taken aback by the similarities of what John and I had witnessed and what Clauson had penned only sixty years after the demise of the factory and village.

I have seen many ghosts in my time, but this particular incident has really stuck out in my mind. Several more trips to Ramtail provided me with fresh air, a light hike and, in some cases, a harsh seasonal chill, but nothing else. I thought that maybe the first time was pure luck and I would never have another paranormal experience at Ramtail, but I was wrong—very wrong.

I decided to take some friends with me who had heard the legend more times than they cared to count. It was time to show them. The four of us hiked the familiar road out to the ruins, where we took our place and began to wait for the glowing form to appear. I told the story one more time in hopes the ghost would hear my recounting and make a showing. This time, the night was clear, and the full moon shone through the trees, creating a natural light along the paths. Since we didn't need flashlights, our night vision would be sharp. I actually feared the moonlight might conflict with the ability to see the glowing night watchman.

After my narration of the legend and my previous experience, we stood quiet. Every so often, we would whisper to one another a few sentences or a small joke about standing in the woods waiting for glowing forms to appear. The silence was suddenly broken by what sounded like the creaking of a lantern swinging to and fro on a handle. I looked around but saw no one within the proximity of the sound. I remember thinking that someone was going to emerge from a bush or from behind a tree with a lantern in one hand and a weapon of some sort in the other, telling us to leave. However, there was no one behind any bush or tree—at least, no one who was still alive. The creaking grew louder as it approached us and moved on toward the remains of what may have been the waste house. We saw no glowing form or even the faint blush that would have been produced by a candle. One must remember once again that there were no kerosene lamps until 1853, thirty-two years after Peleg's demise. Any light that may have been portable was more than likely in the manner of candle lanterns. Candle lanterns had handles much like our modern camping lanterns. Having several lanterns and putting much use to them regularly, I recognized that creaking sound one makes as it swings to and fro from its metal handle.

The creaking next passed to our left, yet we saw no physical body move within the shadows the moon cast on the woods. The noise proceeded to cross the road where the store once stood and then circled around and returned to our right, getting louder as it came close and diminishing in volume as it passed on toward the mill foundation. The creaking coming closer interrupted our whispers once again, passing to our right and slowly dissipating down the old overgrown lane. Whatever it was went one way, and my companions went the other. This would be the first and last time they would accompany me on a ghost hunt.

Legends die hard, and this one had no intention of fading away. My next visit was with my friend Tom Wood. This time it was a cloud-covered, moonless night. One thing is for sure: when darkness falls at Ramtail, it blankets the area with a cloak of black that makes it impossible to see your hand in front of your face without the aid of the moon. This visit was slated for the Round Farm ruins. I wanted to show Tom those remains before heading to the factory. Both sites were easily visited in the course of an evening, and I figured we should start slow and then go for the big finale as far as ghosts were concerned.

The ruins were quite awesome in the early evening twilight. We inspected them, sat for a short vigil and then began back down the path to visit the factory and village. Something happened that I had never experienced there before or since. Tom also remembers vividly what we experienced that evening. Here is his description of what transpired next:

We entered the trail and walked up to the foundations. There was a dirt pile on the side of the road. We took position on the dirt pile and then decided to move to another location on the side of the pile. Tom [D'Agostino] *was just snapping pictures, and he had a recorder going as well. Tom said, "Let's get out of here. We are not going to get anything tonight."*

We began walking back down the trail toward the road. There is a bank on the left with pine trees on it and a field to the right with a stone wall enclosure. We were both walking with our flashlights, and I was probably about ten feet ahead of Tom. I was flashing the light ahead of me as I was walking along, and all of a sudden, I saw wind blowing. All the trees on the right side were bending toward me. I looked to the left, and none of the trees were moving at all. None, literally none. Then all of a sudden, something rushed by me. I got a massive chill, and every hair on this side of my body stood up. I had goose bumps on my right side, the same side where the trees were moving. All I remember Tom saying was, "Did you see that?" As soon as Tom said that, [makes a gesture with his hands] *the flashlight was sky-ground-sky-ground. Tom starts yelling, "Don't run!" so I stop, but I am still sweating bullets because I look back and all the trees behind me were still shaking all the way down the path. They were moving behind Tom, approaching us rapidly. It was about that time when we both decided to get out of there quickly. I did not see what Tom saw, but I did see a little light in the distance. I still get the goose bumps thinking about it.*

I still cannot describe exactly what Tom Wood and I witnessed that night. It looked like a presence almost invisible, yet I could actually see the air move as whatever it was blew by us. It was almost like an old wagon led by horses in full gallop was going by, yet there was no noise. It was a force that overcame the area for those few moments. All I could say was, "I wish I had my camera ready."

Something is obviously still active in that area, as this next account will attest. Susan Wood grew up in the area and picnicked at Ramtail quite frequently with her grandmother. They would often swim at the Barden Reservoir before hiking the roads to Ramtail and the Round Farm. Susan Harrington and Tom Wood were married in 2011. Sue and Tom Wood decided to visit the site at dusk. This is many years after our experience. Here is what Sue shared about their experience:

We were walking in from the Central Pike side. We must have been about three-quarters of the way in when we saw a light going like this [waves her hand back and forth in a semicircular motion] *back and forth. Something was walking the light. It was not a flashlight. Something was carrying it, and you could see by the movement that it was on a hinge or something like that. It looked like wind was blowing, and it was blowing in the wind as whatever it was carried it* [the light]. *The light then vanished into the trees. We were with two other friends, and they did not see it because they were looking another way. We did not want to scare them, so we did not say anything about the light. I never knew about the legends pertaining to the ghostly lantern, but I was very nervous for some reason. The other two friends were ahead of us. All of a sudden, one of them turns around and comes back to us, and she says in a weird voice, "Suzy, don't be afraid of me." She had no recollection of ever saying that. She did not remember anything about that moment when I told her about it later.*

When Tom and Sue Wood first saw the light, it was moving along the side of the large foundation. It then headed toward what was once a field behind a stone wall before vanishing.

Another day, another visit. Actually it was several visits later. Once again, I decided to visit the old Round Farm ruins. I passed Ramtail, quietly muttering, "I'll be back in few," as if someone was already waiting for me to return and pay them a visit. I felt like an amateur archaeologist or something close as I studied the ruins and remains left by previous inhabitants and visitors over the years. This alone kept me going back to both sites. I felt like I needed to dig up the truth, even if I never actually dug up any of the ruins.

On this particular trip, it was a clear warm summer day, and I made my way down the old road as I had many times before. Crossing the stream was an easy task, as the beavers had made quite a dam across the spillway. I began the slight ascent up the old road to the remains of the farm. As I spotted the first wall of the ruins on the left side of the road, I noticed a man wearing heavy farm overalls sitting on the wall. At first I thought nothing of the incident, as Foster is farm country. Then I immediately felt that I may have been on private property but later remembered people fish the river quite often. This became my opportunity to ask a few questions to an old-timer who may have more history in his head than he can remember. I lost sight of him for but a moment as I walked up and rounded a large tree, where I should have come face to face with the old farmer. Instead, I came upon an empty wall. There was absolutely nowhere the man could have gone or moved out of sight in that split second within the sparse wood. He had simply vanished. One second he was there, and in the time it took me to move around a tree, he was gone.

Arlene and I would later visit the farm a few more times and began taking friends legend tripping to the Ramtail site. We even once led a Mini Cooper Club on a haunted tour for a charitable cause on Halloween around the back roads to haunted sites in the area. Forty-eight Mini Coopers rumbled along the old roads, stopping at haunted places to take in the spirit of the season as a fundraiser sponsored by the Ocean State Mini Club. Ramtail, of course, was one of the destinations.

In 2001, Mark Dirrigl wrote a small article in *FATE* magazine regarding his trip to Ramtail. The visit was in response to my article on the haunted factory that appeared in the October 2000 issue of *FATE*. Dirrigl had explored the area, taking photographs before settling down to hold a vigil in the hopes that Peleg might show himself. He would not be disappointed. It appeared the farm site was as haunted as the old mill.

Dirrigl wrote that he began to hear the distinct swinging of a lantern and pointed his camera in the direction of the sound, taking multiple photographs before the noise diminished into the silence. When the pictures were developed, there was a strange glowing form in one of them.

Keith and Sandra Johnson of New England Anomalies Research and the *Ghosts R NEAR* television show have performed many investigations of the site. In fact, Keith and his twin brother, Carl (mentioned later in this chapter), were among the participants when Joe St. Pierre visited and wrote about Ramtail for the *Observer* in 1973. Their experiences at the site, without a doubt, warrant recounting. Here is their story:

An 1885 census for the town of Foster officially lists the Ram Tail Mill as "haunted." Succeeding generations in Foster have continued to keep the legend alive through oral and written tradition. Despite the fact that all that remains of the mill itself is the crumbling foundation, located along a densely wooded path and difficult to find unless one knows exactly where to look, reports of paranormal activity in the area continue to this day. Tom D'Agostino, a local author and paranormal investigator, claims to have recorded the unmistakable creaking sound of a hand held lantern passing directly in front of him. This, of course, was the very type of lantern that Peleg Walker would have carried on his rounds. In 1822, Peleg would have used a candle-illuminated lantern, as opposed to a kerosene lantern. Tom and numerous other explorers have also witnessed bluish, glowing orbs of light floating among the trees in this area at night. My brother Carl, among others, has reported hearing the distant tolling of a bell in this area during the evening hours.

On an evening in August of 2005, I along with several other members of New England Anomalies Research (NEAR) conducted an official investigation at the Ram Tail Site. Tom D'Agostino and his wife Arlene Nicholson accompanied us on this investigation, as well as Denise Jones of Connecticut and author of "The Other Side." Denise's mother Jan Peirce, who frequently assists with investigations and who happens to be somewhat clairvoyant, was in attendance as well. About forty-five minutes into our investigation, Denise's mother announced she had caught a brief glimpse of something—or someone—standing among the dense overgrowth of trees almost directly in front of her. Although it was indistinct, Denise's mother could just barely make out the figure of a tall, thin man dressed in dark clothing, with a rather gaunt expression. She only witnessed this dim figure for a few seconds before it was gone.

Meanwhile, my wife Sandra went to check on the video camera, which she'd set on night vision and placed on a tripod in front of the mill foundation. While checking the camera, she heard the sound of footsteps approaching directly behind her.

Naturally assuming it to be either myself, or one of the other investigators, Sandra said over her shoulder, "I don't know if I'm getting much of anything tonight."

When no one replied, she turned and saw that no one was standing there. After hesitating only for a second or two, Sandra raised her digital camera and snapped a picture. What appeared in the photo was a segmented light streak brightly illuminated against the dark background. Beginning at the top center of the photo, this segmented light streak appears to have been descending at the moment Sandra snapped the picture. The rounded end tip of this light streak actually appears to be luminescent.

More recently on a warm July evening, I and several members of NEAR returned to the Ram Tail area in Foster for a subsequent investigation. During the hike along the rough and overgrown path leading to what was once the mill site, one of our members, Kim, glanced behind and saw what appeared to be a figure following along the trail about thirty yards. Since this was obviously no one who was with our group, she alerted Russ who happened to be beside her. When no one answered them, they halted and called out to whoever it was. The strange thing was, although Kim could clearly make out a pair of legs moving towards them in the gathering darkness, she was unable to see anything else. Russ had just called out for *one of our other members to pass the searchlight to him when the figure silently darted behind a tree, and did not reappear.*

As we continued on along the path, an owl hooted its greeting to us, and a dog could be heard loudly bellowing from somewhere in the far distance. A short time later, after we'd arrived at the site of the Ram Tail Mill foundation, NEAR members Rob and Mike both felt their shirts being tugged, even though no one was close enough to them at the moment to have done so. Rob and Mike also reported to have separately experienced a sudden, cold rush of air against their faces and necks.

The NEAR team also obtained a few examples of Electronic Voice Phenomenon that night. One of the clearer EVPs, captured on audio by team member Kim, seems to be a male voice quietly saying either "Help Peleg" or "Kill Peleg." Another EVP, captured by team member Amie, also sounds like a male voice clearly hissing the word "Bitch."

Just prior to leaving the area that night, we distinctly heard the voices of two men rapidly approaching along the path, and immediately ceased our own conversation to listen. Although we could not decipher exactly what was being said, the voices sounded harsh and angry, as if whoever it was did not like the fact that we were there. We indeed wondered if they were coming to chase us out of the area. Strangely, although we were now in complete darkness, we could see no trace of flashlight beams from our approaching visitors, although they were certainly close enough to do so. And then, to our relief, the voices abruptly faded out, and were not heard by us again that night.

With a touch of humor, Rob asked, "Do you think maybe we scared them off?"

The conclusion seemed to be that what we actually heard were phantom voices, especially since there were no sounds whatsoever of anyone retreating through the brush.

One can only speculate as to the reality of the Ghost of Ram Tail. It would certainly seem that the ghost (or at least the legend) of Peleg Walker, true to his biblical name, did once cause a great deal of division among the residents of the Ram Tail village. The Old Testament name of "Peleg" literally means "divided." Because of Peleg Walker, the once prosperous era of the Ram Tail Mill and Community was forever divided asunder. Does the restless spirit of Peleg Walker continue to roam the mill site, re-enacting his duties as night watchman, while reminding the living of his tragic fate? Or is some other mysterious and unknown force at work there?

Some have theorized that the streams of water from the Ponaganset River running through this area, once harnessed to power the Ram Tail Mill operations, continue to serve as a power source for the paranormal phenomena experienced in this area. This too remains a matter of speculation. Whatever conclusions one may draw, the legacy of the Ram Tail Ghost will most probably endure, for as long as the town of Foster continues to exist.

One important fact I must mention is that Keith and Carl Johnson are not only twins but also distant relatives of Peleg Walker.

One of my most memorable investigations of the area involved a late-night excursion to the Round Farm ruins. It started out with me, Arlene, Andrew Lake of Greenville Paranormal and Andrew's friend Steve Nelson. In May 2007, the nineteenth fell on a Saturday, the perfect day for us working folk to hold an overnight investigation, unless you work on Sunday. At this point, Andrew Lake and I had been conferring back and forth about research we were doing on Ramtail. Just as it had for me, the factory and its legend had become one of Andy's paranormal passions. Andrew, Arlene and I were poised to investigate the area on May 19, but heavy rains dampened our adventure. We decided to postpone the investigation until May 26 and chose the Round Farm for our target due to the recent experiences we both had on separate investigations. It was a hard choice, but there was more excitement happening at the old farm at that point to warrant our decision.

The four of us were to cross the river by the old bridge somehow, but we were not sure how, for the beaver dam that once made crossing effortless had by this time been dismantled. Several previous visits to the site had confirmed this fact, but we were undaunted in our efforts to investigate the old farm. We pulled up to the parking area next to the cemetery at Hopkins Mills, and I was quite surprised to see one of my students and his mother getting out of their SUV with our book *Haunted Rhode Island* in their possession. They were going to check out the old mill based on the book but were very glad to see us. Zack and his mother had taken several excursions to haunted sites contained within the book, and Ramtail was next on their list.

We took them on the tour of the factory and let them know our intentions. Zack expressed how much he would love to join us on an investigation. I told him it was going to be a long one, preferably past midnight, just in case the ghostly bell decided to chime. His mother was more than cordial about the idea of having him join us. "Sure," I said. "We could probably use a few extra hands anyway, and you get to do your first investigation in Rhode Island's officially haunted site."

We invited Zack's mom along, but she had to take care of business at home. Off she went, and away we went down the trail of Ramtail.

Our various attempts to cross the river were no small feat. In fact, it was not going to happen. We ended up transporting everyone in my truck and parking it along the Barden Reservoir side of the property. We then hiked in from there. It was not the actual plan, but we soon found ourselves among the ruins of the farm just as darkness began to set in.

It seemed the Round Farm was the hot spot for ghosts at the time. Perhaps Peleg was taking a breather or he no longer cared to sport his lantern and roam the ruins of the factory. Whatever the case may have been, we were experiencing much of the same at the farm ruins.

The ruins consisted of a small square foundation about the size of a birthing shed. As we traveled a little further, we came upon the remains of what was once a massive barn. The road took a left around the foundation of this barn and directly across on the other side of the old trail was a house foundation and another foundation that may have been another home or some sort of storage. The house foundation was easy to identify by the basement of the central fireplace. Much of the hearth and some of the fireplace were still intact. Sometime in the 1960s, Narragansett Electric acquired the property and placed some poles through the land. There was also a wall with what looked like a built-in fireplace and the last vestiges of a well. Bottles, cans and other implements of old kitchens gone by lay in a heap where the family may have discarded them after use. Bottle dumps were very common before trash pickup in towns, and families reserved places on their properties for such. At some point, the hole would be filled in or the pile covered over, and another one would be started somewhere else. One must remember that this is frugal Yankee territory, so not much was wasted in the first place. Many bottles and other boxes or containers took on other uses.

A small area just within the barn foundation was perfect for unloading our equipment. By now, the sun was almost completely gone, and the nocturnal side of nature began to emerge. Taking readings by flashlight was not a problem as I had performed such a task countless times. We began to hold vigils among the ruins, asking the usual questions. Andy brought a pair of night-vision binoculars, which would later be an invaluable piece of equipment.

Time seemed to fly but strangely enough also stood still. There was a heavy atmosphere that lingered in the air, weighing on our senses. It was almost as if we were among many people, yet we could see no one. Suddenly, Andy was seeing something. It moved quickly and vanished. What appeared to be some sort of light came and went. The light resembled a candle moving through the woods. Staring and standing motionless, we peered into the darkness, taking turns with the night-vision binoculars in hopes of seeing something, even if it was not paranormal, that would explain the eerie glow that had so quickly come and gone. Our eyes were now accustomed to the night, but as usual, it was extremely dark, despite the presence of a moon. As time went by, we decided to set up down the path past the foundations heading toward the old bridge. It was close to midnight, and we still hoped to hear the bell.

Up the path in front of the foundations, we thought we saw something moving. It appeared to be someone crossing the overgrown lane as if going from the old home to check on the barn. Even without the night-vision binoculars, we could see the vague figure in the distance, as that portion of land was where two old roads intersected. This left an opening through the trees to see the night sky, which dimly lit that small piece of the woods and the lane. We entertained the idea that it could have been our eyes, tired from straining in the dark, or trees swaying in the breeze creating what looked like human motion. But we all saw it. It was there. It crossed back toward the home. I also whispered to the group that the trail turned toward Route 6, spilling out onto the little Rounds Lane. Maybe one of the residents from there heard us and sought to check out what we were doing in the woods at such a late hour. I took the initiative to walk back to the foundations, figuring I would see or hear someone moving about. Perhaps they were waiting for us, as our equipment was still in the barn ruins. When I reached the ruins, several yards from where we were holding vigil, there was no one.

It was well past midnight when we packed up and headed out. We never heard the bell, but we did have some strange experiences. Although not hardcore and definitive, they made for a night to remember.

Although Ramtail at night was as eerie as you could ever want to experience, day vigils became more prominent for Arlene and me. We had performed several investigations at night with no results, so we figured we would give the place a try during late afternoon into twilight. Some of our evidence was quite startling.

Arlene and I took her daughter, Mandy, along during one of these investigations at the factory and village. We had at that point become partial to investigating the factory as opposed to the farm due to the new evidence we had uncovered in regard to Peleg's "sudden death." The fact that the other property was on watershed land and supposedly off limits was a catalyst to stay away as well. We chose to respect the signs that were suddenly put up along the edge of the woods and concentrated on the one place I really felt should be investigated more anyway: Ramtail Factory.

The three of us situated ourselves within the remains of the factory and began our vigil. Two recorders were set up, along with two video cameras. Arlene is a gifted tarot card reader. In our investigations, we use the cards to help field questions we may otherwise never think to ask. There is a good reason for this, and it came from this session at the mill.

During an EVP session, it became clear that we might not be in communication with Peleg Walker. The cards leaned toward a female presence in the way they were falling. The first card told of a woman, and the next told of some unexpected incident that changed her life. While this combination of cards may have been typical, Arlene drew a card and, knowing the meaning of the card, asked who was the woman in charge of finances. After the reading, we asked a few more questions and invited any presence to join us in our conversation before packing up.

The reading may have had little effect on us at the time, but when I played the recording later, right after Arlene asked about the woman in charge of the finances, a whispery voice blurted out, "Orra Potter." We both stared in disbelief, for, as we knew, when Olney Potter died suddenly on May 15, 1831, his wife, Orra, was left with most of the shares in the factory.

Mandy accompanied us again on her next visit. We tried the same setup with the tarot and recorders as before. The reading came out differently, but our equipment was ready to capture any and everything. The day began to wane, and as we continued our investigation, Mandy wandered off to the left of the old wheel race to explore the outer perimeter of the mill. That is when it happened. A thunderous splash into the river made all three of us jump and blurt out one curse or another. In an instant, all was quiet. I was the first to move toward the noise. Nervously watching, Arlene and Mandy began to laugh when I announced that a beaver had decided to let us know of its presence by slapping the water with its tail. The score was beaver, one; ghost hunters, zero.

On May 19, Arlene and I took a trek out to Ramtail. This would be the third time I had visited the little hamlet on that particular date. Each time, I was hoping for some monumental paranormal event to transpire, but each time, the spirits decided that they were not in the mood for company. As J. St. Pierre put it in his 1973 article for the *Observer*, "I felt sure we would get results. Such was not the case. There was no nocturnal ringing, no clatter and whirr of machinery…nor any ghostly manifestations."

I must divulge that it later occurred to me that the haunting did not start until about a week after Peleg's death, so it would have been better to pay the area a visit several days after the nineteenth. And, as you may have guessed, Arlene and I have done so several times.

On any given afternoon, it would be a fun adventure to take someone to Ramtail and perform a vigil for about a half hour or so. It is uncanny how you can feel the energy in the air when the spirits are there and the lack of them when they are not tenanting the area. I am not saying it is a negative essence by any means. In all cases, the aura of Ramtail is tranquil and pervading with a peaceful overtone, but then there is that other feeling that creeps up on you. It is an exhilarating, energized feeling that comes over you when the spirits are present that heightens your senses almost instinctively.

It is the same feeling Arlene and I felt when we decided to hold a late Sunday afternoon vigil at the mill ruins on the fourth Sunday in May 2012, a week and one day after the anniversary of Peleg Walker's death. I set a few hand-held cameras in strategic places, started the recorder and took my position in the ruins of the factory. Arlene, as usual, shuffled the cards until they felt ready and began to distribute them into the usual formation on the ground.

We asked questions based on the meanings of the cards drawn from the deck. The cards fell in a succession of similar readings as previously performed at the ruins: a struggle, finances, business, tragedy and death. These are common to many readings, but each new reading seemed to become more precise and more focused on the subject than the previous readings. One of the cards indicated treachery or foul play. I directly asked Peleg if he had an argument with the Potters that ended badly. I would later hear a faint but distinct "yes" when I played the recording. One of the questions I asked shortly after was, "What happened on the night of May 19, 1822?"

The next few seconds of playback sent the hairs on my arms and neck skyward. One word, distinct and audible came through: "Killed."

What do you make of an answer such as that?

I have always said ghost hunting is like fishing. A little luck and the right "bait," coupled with some patience and experience, and you just might have a good day. While fishing a river such as the Ponaganset, anglers will naturally try different locations along the banks in hopes of casting where the fish are biting. The same holds true for the Ramtail area. Do we want to investigate the mill, the farm, the pool or all three? Decisions, decisions. I cannot help but feel extra disappointment when we leave Ramtail with no paranormal experiences. It is the feeling that we chose to investigate the wrong place at the wrong time. The ghosts may be hollerin' it up at the old farmstead while we are sitting patiently at the mill for nothing. Arlene and I will attest to one fact: regardless of whether the ghosts make a showing, Ramtail is an alluring parcel of land where time seems to stand still, and all your worries at present seem to fade away, at least for a while.

I received a call from our friend and EVP expert Michael "Mike" Markowicz. Novelist and screenwriter Jennifer B. White had decided to do an independent film on electronic voice phenomena and cast Mike for the lead role because of his research and experiments in the field. They were interested in doing a segment on Ramtail and wanted us to take him there. On a cool Sunday afternoon, Arlene and I met Mike and Jennifer at Shady Acres, a famous local Foster restaurant that has been in business longer than anyone can actually remember. From there, Ramtail was only a few miles east. As we pulled into the parking area adjacent to the Hopkins Mills Cemetery, I felt a rush of excitement, but I always do at Ramtail. Arlene and I brought my massive binder full of everything we had on the history and haunt of the factory so we could fill them in on what to expect as we traversed the old lane leading to the ruins. They could also photograph any documents that might have been important to the film. Once we arrived, Mike set out to do what he does best: capture EVPs. Arlene began reading the cards, and I asked a few pertinent questions to get the dialogue moving. Mike and I both had our Edison boxes with us, and I trained mine on an AM frequency while Mike chose FM. One of us was going to get lucky. It would be Mike. During one of the sessions, he captured a voice that said, "Peleg." What are the odds that name would randomly come across a radio? Evidence such as that can really sway a person's opinion about a reputed haunt. It certainly made Mike and Jennifer think twice.

Another film project, the *Haunted Rhode Island* documentary, a three-part series, was a lot of fun to be a part of. My song "Ramtail" was used in the film. I was asked to be of assistance with the project because of my research and long history of visiting the place. Jason Mayoh, Brian Harnois and Christian White, all respected artists in their field, had put together a show for Rhode Island Public Broadcast System, and I was now working on the series, thanks to my first book, *Haunted Rhode Island*. They met at our house to film some shots of me going over the documents I had on Ramtail. It was during this filming that they got a little more than they bargained for.

While the camera was rolling, a shade decided to fly up and slam against the windowsill. This has never happened before, nor has it happened since with any of the window shades in the house. They were startled, but the best was yet to come: the nighttime investigation of the Ramtail Factory.

The usual equipment was transported to the site, as well as special audio and video for the show. Special lights for night filming were set up, as we were well aware darkness was to be our foremost hindrance. The night was cloudy, and rain threatened to break any moment. It was not the precipitation that had everyone nervous as much as the darkness. Again the pitch-black condition was so intense that we literally could not see one inch in front of us. Good thing for powerful flashlights. Christian had much to say about the black veil that covered the woods. We were about to begin when we heard a noise coming from the direction of the old mill home ruins. The din startled Jay, Brian and Christian, but I knew better. My friend Rich Allarie was coming to join us, and in the rush to set up for the filming, I forgot to inform them of his later arrival.

With all of us ready to go, we commenced our investigation for the film. Brian repeatedly commanded Peleg to show himself while we kept our light trained on anything that might be of interest. One of the first signs that something was going to happen was that the batteries in Jay and Christian's equipment drained extremely fast. They swore they had put fresh cells in and charged all the equipment, which should have lasted three hours, not fifteen minutes. I had my hand-held camera, a decent one with night vision and an extra battery. That would have to do for the rest of the filming.

We set ourselves up along the edge of the ruins and began to hold vigil, once again calling for Peleg Walker. A small light began to move about the trees through the darkness. We all saw it almost simultaneously. I could feel the tense excitement that began to flow through all of us as we watched this dim glow move slowly, swaying to and fro along the edge of the road. From what little we could see around the glow, there was no physical form of any sort holding the light as it moved along the lane. There was also no sound being made by the holder of the light. The dim glow slowly moved by the ruins of the store toward us. It was an orange and yellow glow that appeared to flicker as it moved. The excitement of this phenomenon had us going. Jason exclaimed, "Can you see it? Can you see it? Get it on video!" A tree was obstructing my view as I zeroed in on the light. The night vision on the camcorder made it extremely difficult to see the light. Turning the option off only proved futile in the extreme dark of the woods. Turning it on made everything glow to the point where it was difficult to see the flickering light moving up the path. Andrew Lake compared it to trying to see into the darkness beyond a campfire. I proceeded to move forward and almost fell face first off the rock. I had forgotten that I perched myself on a large boulder. In the darkness, I could see absolutely nothing and was not aware of my present position until I fell, missing the moving light almost completely. So much for the finesse of an experienced investigator.

On October 5, 2008, Carl Johnson—with his girlfriend, Laura Casey, and Andrew Lake—investigated the site. Carl is the twin brother of Keith Johnson. The two made their first appearance at Ramtail during the 1973 investigation by Joe St. Pierre. This was for the aforementioned article that appeared in the *Observer* that same year. Having paid many visits to the site from the early 1970s to present, if anyone had a history with investigating Ramtail, it would be Carl and Keith.

Here is his story:

> *I had a kind of eerie feeling that someone was watching me, but that is what I expect because we were out at a reported haunted site.*
>
> *I was walking near what was reported to be the ruins near a square configuration [the wheel race] and a pathway. Laura and I were wandering now with a flashlight with us. We had separated from Andrew and his companion, and I turned to look back down the path. I saw coming toward me, what appeared to be an orange torch or lantern flame. This was about five feet above the ground over the path. It was orange and yellow, but it was a flame. It was making kind of an "S" configuration and floating over the path. I saw this for about three seconds, and then it was gone. It was not swamp gas or anything I could account for. It did not fade away, [snaps his fingers] just gone. Laura did not see it, I wish I had someone to corroborate the experience but it was just I who saw it that night. Then I heard some other people had seen a flame traveling down that path and witnesses describe it the same way. What everyone describes is basically an "S" configuration that floats over the path. It is orange and yellow but it is quite definite when you see it, especially since it is dark in those woods. It was probably 8:30 p.m. at the time I saw it.*

Two years previous, Carl had paid a visit to Ramtail and, at 9:45 p.m., heard a bell ring three times. There is no church or fire station in the immediate area of the factory or farm ruins. Why it would toll three times became an enigma to Carl. He has related this experience to me over and over to the point where I want to spend nights at Ramtail just to hear the phantom bell.

If anyone has some experiences to share, it would be Andrew Lake of Greenville Paranormal in Greenville, Rhode Island. Andrew and I grew up in the same neighborhood in the sleepy little village a few miles east of Foster, and he is well respected in the field of the paranormal. Andrew has researched the mill and its haunts for seven years as of this writing. His findings have been a valuable asset in the telling of Ramtail from many aspects. Andrew had his own experience that evening while waiting for Carl and Laura to arrive at the mill. Andrew was preparing for the nighttime vigil when he suddenly spied a ball of light across the river next to the granite marker in front of the dam ruins. As he recalls:

> It was an intense little ball of light. It appeared for about five seconds and was gone. I fired up my recorder to see if I could get some EVPs. Before I could ask "What is your name?" I distinctly heard a breathy voice say, "Cole." I recorded for a few minutes and when I played the messages back, there was someone singing on the recorder. John Hardy [a fellow investigator and EVP specialist] cleaned and processed the recording so I could hear what it was saying…it was someone in a singsong voice saying, [impersonates the voice on the recording] "I feel sorry, I can't take it no more." Both of us were stunned by the recording.

Andrew has seen the light four separate times at various times of the year under different weather conditions and hours. One evening in May 2009, he ran across some teenagers walking through the site. They started a conversation about the factory and its ghosts. The teenagers told Andrew they had seen the eerie light one night while visiting Ramtail. They mentioned that the incident lasted about five seconds, and then the light was gone. This parallels other eyewitness accounts of the phantom light. Andrew asked the teens to point in the direction they had witnessed the phenomenon. It was no surprise to him that they all pointed to the same spot where Andrew, Arlene, myself and others have beheld the ghostly lantern glow.

There is an account of two Foster police officers who were on patrol one night and experienced the phantom tolling. According to the story, the officers were on their usual shift, driving around the area of Hopkins Mills where basically nothing ever happens, when they heard the pealing of a bell. One officer joked to the other that it was probably the haunted mill bell. Though they were very close to the church situated in Hopkins Mills, they decided it was not coming from that old meetinghouse. The faint tolling was coming from somewhere south of Hopkins Mills but within proximity. They quickly headed down Ram Tail Road, where the sound of the last few signals of the bell could be heard in the direction of the mill ruins. They had heard the ghostly pealing of the mill bell. The time recorded was 10:00 p.m. Another patrolman once spotted Andrew heading into the woods toward the factory ruins. While conversing about the haunting Andrew remembers the officer saying that he has his cruiser and a gun and would still never venture into the woods of Ramtail alone in the dark.

Lifelong resident Stan Hopkins once attested to hearing the clang of the ghost bell breaking the late-night silence in the distant woods near the old mill village. Pat Morgan, a resident of the area since the 1950s, once heard the bell toll. She went outside to feed her pigs at dawn when she suddenly heard the pealing of a bell emanating from the direction of the old Ramtail mill. She had lived there for about ten years before that and had previously never heard the din. She then remembered that the night watchman would ring the bell at dawn to summon the workers to the factory.

These two residents are not alone. Scores of old-timers residing in the Hopkins Mills section of town have either experienced the ethereal ringing or have heard someone else's story of the bell that once woke the workers of the Foster Woolen Manufacturing Co. but now reminds the residents of the ghost that forever haunts the land now called Ramtail.

The haunting of the Ramtail Factory is not complete without including the story of the swimming hole just below the small wooden bridge that spans the Ponaganset River on Ramtail Road. Originally, the pool was much larger and deeper than is witnessed today. When the dam for the factory was still somewhat functional, the pool was the meeting place for all the children in the area. According to Richard Hopkins, the swimming hole looked like the Mississippi when he was a child. He went on to state, "Everyone went there and for a good reason. A lot of people didn't have bathtubs, and you went down there and actually took a bath."

Many of the locals will often recount tales of enjoyable moments spent at the Ramtail swimming hole, but not all reminiscences were pleasant. Francis Bellows Harrington was swimming with her best friend when suddenly the girl (last name Blanchard) began to struggle. From atop the bridge used as a

A church at Hopkins Mills, complete with bell and tower. *Photo courtesy of the Foster Preservation Society.*

diving platform for the pool, young Francis saw something white just below the surface in the water pulling her friend under. She quickly dove into the water, pulling her friend to safety. Mrs. Harrington could never explain what exactly she saw that day, but she knew it resembled someone in a white dress pulling at the other girl, trying to drag her under the surface of the swimming hole.

The RamTail Guest

The Foster Preservation Society presents the eighth in its series of tours of historical landmarks and scenic areas in Foster. It is our hope that readers will become better acquainted with our town through these tours.

Near this spot about 100 years ago stood the Ram Tail Spinning Mill. One morning when the factory door was opened, workers were greeted with the body of a partner, swinging from the rafters. Death by suicide. About midnight, on the third day after the death, villagers were awakened by the toll of the mill bell. When brave workers entered the mill, the bell became silent. This happening was repeated for the next few days. Only the complete destruction of the bell stopped this penomenon. A few nights later mill workers found the wheel running backwards in the abnormally placid waters. Workers quit and went to work elsewhere. Soon after, the mill burned down and the village of Ram Tail disappeared. Now the ghost presides over a deep, peaceful swimming hole.

—Foster Preservation Society Photo

Left: This small write-up and photo of the Ramtail ghost and swimming hole states, "Near this spot about 100 years ago stood the Ramtail Spinning Mill… now the ghost presides over a deep, peaceful swimming hole." *Photo courtesy of the Foster Preservation Society.*

Below: The bridge on Rams Tail Road overlooking the haunted swimming hole.

90

There are other eyewitness accounts of a strange mist rising from the pool and slowly taking a human form. Witnesses state that the phenomenon takes place in the summer just before dark. There are no documented drownings at the pool, but that does not mean the pool or river is untainted by such a tragedy. There is a story of a woman who put stones in her pocket and walked into the pool. It is told that the girl in white haunting the pool was her daughter. This is legend, of course, with no known records to prove such an incident ever took place.

CHAPTER 8

OTHER LOCAL HAUNTS

I saw a visage from the past
It came to me in full moonlight
It spoke, "I am not the last,
For there are more with me this night."
—*Thomas D'Agostino*

The next few local ghost stories are closely related to Ramtail. There are several tales of witches and strange characters around Ramtail and Hopkins Mills that have etched themselves into the history of Foster. Here are some of those stories.

Dorothy "Dolly" Ellen Cole (December 9, 1769–June 13, 1860) would have been proud to know that the hill overlooking her home was named after her, as was the bridge spanning what was once known as the Round Hill River. The waterway is now called Dolly Cole Brook. The legend that surrounds her is quite a different story. Somewhere along the line of history, Dolly Cole has become known as a witch, vampire, cross-dressing murder victim and a ghost that haunts the Hopkins Mills Historic District, just north of Ramtail.

Her ghost may haunt the area, but the legends that have surfaced about her life are interesting as well. Here are the tales of Dolly Cole that have been told around flickering campfires and in publications over the years.

Dolly Cole was a twenty-seven-year-old woman who took a liking to wearing men's clothing. She worked at her uncle's blacksmith forge, not far from her home, and she often took a shortcut through the woods near

Tucker Hollow Road on the Foster/Scituate border to get to her uncle's forge. One summer day in 1893, while walking through the woods, she was accosted and murdered near the swamp along a section of Tucker Hollow Road. It was a tragic incident that left the little hamlet in shock. To make matters worse, the murderer was never found. To this day, her ghost, most likely in search of justice, is seen in the area of the swamp where she was murdered. The Cranston Rod and Gun Club owns a portion of the property where she is seen, so wandering through the woods in search of her ghost is not advised, as club members are often practicing at the firing range.

I have spoken with several members of the club about the legend, and although they were familiar with the story, none of the members interviewed have ever seen the cross-dressing ghost. The story never made the papers, and any other records that may have been kept at the time make no mention of a Dolly Cole being murdered. Upon researching the name, I found that only one Dorothy "Dolly" Ellen Cole ever existed in Foster. Of course, she died in 1860 at ninety-one years, six months and four days. I was later informed that this story was made up and widely spread by a local trying to gain publicity as a ghost hunter.

Some say that Dolly Cole was a witch and the townsfolk, fearing her powers, set her home ablaze to rid her from their hamlet. When she came running out with her young infant in her arms, one of the vigilantes grabbed her child and threw the baby over the bridge into the Ponaganset River. The woman jumped over the edge of the span into the river to save her baby, but neither was ever seen again. Since then, her ghost roams the area, haunting the families of those who caused her death. There are also stories that claim she was not a witch but a vampire. The next story tells of the ghost of Dolly Cole haunting the bridge near her former home. This is the first story I ever heard about the legend.

Dolly Cole, a tavern keeper, often ran up the steep hill near her home to catch a glimpse of the stagecoach that would run through Hopkins Mills, stopping at the tavern. Legend says she drowned in the Ponaganset River while attempting to fill her pail with water from the rushing stream. Her ghost has been seen since walking the Old Danielson Pike that cuts through Hopkins Mills Historic District. Many people have seen her standing near the bridge at the edge of the stream that both bear her name. She has been witnessed by many of the people who live in the homes along Old Danielson Pike.

Those who I interviewed have seen her ethereal form moving along the edge of the river toward the pool where she met her demise. One

The Providence-Danielson stagecoach ran through Hopkins Mills. *Photo courtesy of the Foster Preservation Society.*

couple saw her several times in their yard. Each time they saw her, she was wearing a white dress and carrying a wooden bucket. They could tell she was not human because she looked almost like a "projection being played," according to the wife, who also said she "seemed to float" across the property. I tend not to doubt any of the stories, as I have a firsthand account of the ghost of Dolly Cole.

It was in the autumn of 1972. My father and I went fishing at the Ponaganset River in Foster. Hopkins Mills Pond still acts as a resting point for the river as it flows through the pond and down the remains of a dam before it forms a pool and continues across Route 6 toward Ramtail. The Hopkins Mills Fishing Area affords ample parking and a small boat launch for a canoe or raft. This was the site of the former Simmons Braid Mill. The remains of the mill still sit amid the brush and bramble. My father was an avid trout fisherman, and I, of course, just threw my line in the water and hoped for the catch of a lifetime, which, as usual, never happened.

We came to the pool just past the remains of the old Simmons Braid Mill, where the river flowed under the Ponaganset River Bridge that was once part of the Old Danielson Pike. This bridge is about a quarter of a mile from the Dolly Cole Bridge. The Dolly Cole Brook is but a minute stream compared to the flowing waters of the Ponaganset River. Besides, the Ponaganset River is the water that is stocked with trout during the fishing season.

The Dolly Cole Bridge on Old Danielson Pike in Hopkins Mills. *Photo courtesy of the Foster Preservation Society.*

The Old Simmons Braid Mill in Hopkins Mills was located where the present fishing area now sits. The mill was just above the pool where the author witnessed the ghost of Betsey Grayson. *Photo courtesy of the Foster Preservation Society.*

My father let me cast my line in the east side of the pool while he crossed the river and took the west side. Crossing the river at one point is effortless, as the boulders from the old dam create a natural bridge to get back and forth from one side to the other.

After several minutes and no hits on our lines, my father yelled over to me that he was going to move a few yards downstream and walked out of sight within the brush along the bank. The swirling waters gushed over the rocks, creating a serene resonance along the banks of the river, one that made you relax and daydream of the peace and quiet that pervaded the area. At that point, a fish could have taken my bait, line, rod and reel from my hands, and I would not have acknowledged the fact until much later. The scenery had entranced me.

My reverie was suddenly disrupted by the presence of a woman who appeared on the other side of the pool. I could not help but stare at the woman, as something was very peculiar about her appearance. She was dressed in a long white gown, much heavier than the season should have afforded, and she wore no shoes. She moved slowly, almost forlornly, to the edge of the pool and dipped an old wooden bucket into the water. She never paid me any mind, as if she was not aware of any presence. At first, I began to wonder where we really were. How far out in the boonies had my father taken us where people look like they are still living in the nineteenth century?

As I watched her dip the bucket, I began to notice that she did not appear to be "real." It was like I was watching an image being projected onto the scenery. She then took her bucket and moved down the path in the direction my father had gone. A few moments later, my father emerged, and I asked him if he had seen the strange-looking woman carrying a bucket. He assured me he had not seen anyone pass by him. The brush and trees, being so thick, would not allow anyone to move off the path, yet their sparseness still afforded good visibility through the woods. I passed it off as being in a strange place for the first time and never thought about it again until a year later.

Just in time for Halloween, the *Observer* ran articles of ghost stories and legends pertaining to Rhode Island, namely the towns of Scituate, Smithfield, Glocester and Foster. That is when I read about the famous ghosts of Dolly Cole and Ramtail.

Many years later, I decided to really look into the ghost of Dolly Cole. The whole history was already at my fingertips, and using my records, all I needed to do was to put it all in a timeline. This is when something else came to light. After purchasing Margery Matthews's pamphlet on the factory and

The pool below Hopkins Mills Pond is where the ghost of Betsey was seen dipping her wooden bucket into the water.

Peleg Walker, I made a startling discovery: the ghost of Dolly Cole was not Dolly Cole.

Toward the back of the publication, there is a mention of Betsey Grayson (also spelled Betsey Greyson):

> *An elderly woman in poor circumstances lived in one of the shabby houses. One day, carrying her bucket, she went to the Ponaganset River where she got her supply of water. As she leaned forward to fill the bucket, she slipped, lost her footing, and unable to regain her balance, tumbled into the river. The body of 74 year-old Betsey A. Grayson who drowned on December 29, 1860 was found in a swamp meadow where it had been carried by the swift current. Possibly she had worked at the factory and had been allowed to remain in one of the cottages. Her accidental drowning strengthened the belief that the village was haunted.*

This explains a lot of aspects of the Dolly Cole legend. The details surrounding Betsey Grayson's drowning were more than likely presumed and therefore could have been altered by storytellers to fit a more sinister tone. The fact that she was found in the swamp meadow also coincides with the story of Dolly Cole being murdered near a swamp. The main fact that she was found near the Cole property also adds impetus to the reason why the name may have been altered over the telling.

One further article found by researcher and paranormal investigator Andrew Lake helped solidify the fact that the ghost seen around Ramtail and Hopkins Mills is that of Betsey Grayson. That was the aforementioned 1948 *Windham County Transcript* article written by Clara Wade Clemence about the Ramtail haunt. Clemence wrote, "A Mrs. Grayson who lived in one of the tenements went to get water when the stream was high. Her pail that she put into the rushing current pulled her into the river. Her body was found down the stream in a swamp meadow." The ghost of Betsey Grayson has been often referred to as the "Woman in White" and is witnessed to this day.

I find it odd no one has connected Betsey Grayson's ghost to the swimming hole haunt. It would make sense since the pool is not far from where she fell

Record of Betsey Grayson's death by drowning. Note where it states, "Drowned."

Plaque marking the original Dolly Cole Bridge on Old Danielson Pike in Hopkins Mills.

into the water and was found. It was also very close to the old cottages where she resided as a squatter. With such physical ties to the area, it would seem logical that her ghost would still roam between Ramtail and Hopkins Mills, as her mortal frame once did.

As for the real Dorothy Ellen Cole, she married Hugh Cole, who died on July 25, 1819, at the age of sixty-two years, twenty-seven days. Mr. Cole served in the military, reaching the rank of colonel. His stone is marked accordingly. Buried next to Hugh and Dorothy is their son, Hugh Cole, and his wife, Nancy. The Cole name is prominent in this part of Foster, and Hugh Cole's property once abutted that of Peleg Walkers. The reader may be wondering why I bother to give a few details of the Cole family in this writing. For history's sake alone, such mention should be included, but this next fact is much more important to the story of Ramtail: Orra Potter's maiden name was Cole. She was the daughter of Dorothy and Hugh Cole. Orra, Olney and a few of their children are buried close by the Cole lot.

It is easy to get Dolly Cole confused with others who may have possessed special talents or stood out among the rural folk of Foster. For instance, Isiah

Brown of Hopkins Mills married Peggy Hurley (or Herlihy) of Ireland. She was renowned for her spells and herbal remedies. Isiah died in 1897 and is buried in Foster Cemetery No. 034. Peggy may be buried there, but it is not on record, though there exist among the carved monuments several stones with no inscriptions. Not far from Hopkins Mills, at the Rhode Island/Connecticut border, lived two women known to be witches. Abby and Whaley Brown were called the "witches of Jerimoth Hill." The two sisters were feared far and wide for their ability to cast spells and cause items to fly about rooms. They are buried in Foster Cemetery No. 001 on the Rhode Island/Connecticut border. Abby was born in 1803 and died in 1875, but there is no Whaley Brown mentioned in the records. I researched to see if Whaley was a married name, and it is not. I have visited the cemetery on a few occasions but do not remember seeing a Whaley Brown among the stones. There is a Phila Brown born in 1805 and died in 1880, and a Pardon Brown born in 1792 and died in 1869 who would have been about the same age as Abby. Whatever the case, the two sisters were known as witches almost into the twentieth century and are still subjects of Halloween stories in the town.

Just east of Hopkins Mills on Route 6 sits the entrance to Tucker Hollow Road. This mostly gravel road appears unchanged over the centuries. Although there are some newer homes along the road, there is one place that has not seen construction for centuries—and for good reason. This little parcel of land is called the Ghost Lot.

Aunt Lonnie Davis was known as a recluse. Some claim she was a witch who lived on Tucker Hollow Road. Lonnie would push her cart down Route 6 to Hopkins Mills, where she would procure her necessities and then push the full cart back up the steep hill heading toward home. Never once did she ever accept any assistance from the local gentry. It is related that she seemed to have an aversion to the townsfolk so serious that when she died, she demanded that her home be demolished and never rebuilt. It was a strange request with an even stranger consequence. It was said that if so much as two boards remained nailed together, she would haunt the area until her wish was granted in full.

When Aunt Lonnie died, the townspeople failed to adhere to her demand and soon paid the price for their actions. Whenever someone passed by the abandoned property, screams could be heard from the home, and a cold breath would send a chill down their backs. If anyone dared venture onto the cursed land, a voice would whisper in his ear, and the cold air would send him fleeing for safer ground.

It came to pass that the only way the neighbors could be rid of Aunt Lonnie was to fulfill her last wish. The home was torn down, and no two boards remained nailed together—or so they thought. The land where Lonnie Davis once lived is now called the Ghost Lot and continues to be haunted centuries later. There is a foundation where the home once stood, and the land has not yet been rebuilt on.

Mary Davis and her husband, Joseph, are buried in the Tucker Hollow Cemetery, very close to the Ghost Lot. Perhaps Aunt Lonnie was a nickname given to Mary; Lonnie could have been her middle name. Her birth date is unknown, but her death date of 1799 is clearly marked on the rough stone that sits among the brush and growth in the old burying yard. As for the Ghost Lot, it is not recommended to venture there alone or after dark, for Aunt Lonnie is still watching over her property and is not cordial to strangers.

The ghosts hold vigil in the night
Their glowing eyes cause many a fright
With lantern or bucket in their hand
They eternally wander the wooded land.
—Thomas D'Agostino

CONCLUSION

Despite all the stories, experiences, research and documentation, this is a story with no definite conclusion. We may never know all the facts pertaining to the people and the ghosts of Ramtail. There is no one left living to give us the intimate details that time has so conveniently misted into hazy legends.

I am confident that as the years pass, more tidbits of facts will surface in regard to the history of Ramtail, like the stones on a New England farm that mysteriously appear after the spring thaw.

Who haunts the Round Farm? Was it actually part of the Ramtail mill village? Does the ghost of more than one person haunt the mill ruins? There may never be an accurate answer to who hanged himself or who cut his own throat. In the end, all we can do is continue to ask into the wind in hopes of answers that will eliminate all doubt about what actually occurred at Ramtail a long, long time ago.

Under low arched bridges through the alder thicket
Past the tumbling ruin of the haunted mill
Where the ghosts and goblins hold their midnight revel.
And the forms of suicides the passers' blood will thrill…
—*Marcia Hopkins Barden from "The Ponaganset River," 1884*

A Brief Chronological History of Peleg Walker and the Ramtail Factory

1787	Peleg Walker is born.
1810	Peleg Walker marries Mary "Polly" Potter.
1813	The Foster Woolen Manufacturing Company is established.
1816	Peleg Walker buys land adjacent to the company property.
1821	Peleg Walker purchases two small mills, a cotton factory and some land in Burrillville, Rhode Island.
1822	Peleg Walker sells half his share in the Burrillville investment to William A. Potter.
1822	Peleg Walker is found dead of an apparent suicide.
1822	David Wilkinson purchases most of Peleg Walker's interests in land and property.
1823	David Wilkinson sells his shares of Ramtail to Olney E. Potter.
1824	Marvin Round sells his shares to Olney E. Potter.
1827	Jonathon Ellis sells his shares to Olney E. Potter.
1831	Olney E. Potter dies suddenly.
1843	William A. Potter dies, leaving Orra and Catherine Potter as owners of the factory.
1844	Orsumus Taft of Uxbridge, Massachusetts, purchases all rights and shares to Ramtail.
1847	Welcome Arnold purchases property.
1848–59	Factory production ceases.
1859	Richard Briggs acquires Ramtail.

1860	Betsey Grayson, a reported squatter of one of the Ramtail cottages, drowns in the Ponaganset River while fetching a bucket of water.
1867	John D. Cranston owns Ramtail.
1873	Factory burns to its foundation.
1881	George Burnham purchases the land.
1885	Burnham sells Ramtail to the Barden Reservoir Company for one dollar.
1885	Amos Perry labels Ramtail as "haunted" on page 36 of the Rhode Island State Census.
1900	Barden Reservoir Company transfers the land to the Providence Water Supply Board.
1927	Providence Water Supply Board sells Ramtail to Frank Hinckley for ten dollars.
1937	James Earl Clauson writes about the Ramtail ghost in his book *These Plantations*.
1948	Clara Wade Clemence writes about the Ramtail ghost for the *Windham County Transcript*.
1961	Lytle Hopkins writes about the Ramtail Haunting for the *Observer* newspaper.
1972	Thomas D'Agostino witnesses the ghost of Betsey Grayson in Hopkins Mills.
1973	Joe St. Pierre writes article "Ghosts at Ramtail?" for the *Observer* newspaper.
1978	Hinckley sells land to Helfgott and Blinkhorn.
1980	Margery Matthews writes the pamphlet *Peleg's Last Word: The Story of the Foster Woolen Manufactory.*
1992	Lucy Corporation acquires Ramtail.
1992	*Old Rhode Island* magazine, *Providence Journal Bulletin* and the *Observer* all publish articles on Ramtail.
1992	Thomas D'Agostino begins investigations and research on Ramtail.
1995	*Providence Journal* publishes another small story on Ramtail.
2000	Thomas D'Agostino publishes a full-length article on the Ramtail haunting for *FATE* magazine.
2003	The story of Ramtail from Thomas D'Agostino's manuscript "Curious New England" is used by Susan Smitten for her book *Ghost Stories of New England.*
2005	Thomas D'Agostino writes a chapter on Ramtail for the book *Encyclopedia of Haunted Places,* compiled by Jeff Belanger.

2006   Ramtail appears in the book *Haunted Rhode Island*.

2007   Ramtail appears in the book *Abandoned Villages and Ghost Towns of New England*.

2008   Ramtail becomes a land trust for all to enjoy.

2009   Arlene Nicholson and Thomas D'Agostino hold many investigations and extensive research on Ramtail and Peleg Walker.

2009   Ramtail becomes part of the documentary *Things That Go Bump in the Night: Tales of Haunted New England*.

2011   Ramtail is featured in the documentary *Haunted Rhode Island*, based on the book by Thomas D'Agostino and Arlene Nicholson.

2012   Dolly Cole and Aunt Lonnie Davis are featured in the second documentary of *Haunted Rhode Island*.

2013   Ramtail is featured in the book *Legends, Lore and Secrets of New England*.

2014   The first full-length book on Ramtail, written by Thomas D'Agostino and Arlene Nicholson, is published.

BIBLIOGRAPHY

Arnold, James. *Vital Records of Rhode Island, 1636–1850.* Providence, RI: Narragansett Historical Publishing Co., 1891.

Benson, Virginia I. *Churches of Foster.* N.p.: Webster Printing Co., 1978.

Boisvert, Donald J. "Rhode Island Vampires, Eerie Spirits, and Ghostly Apparitions." *Old Rhode Island* 2, issue 9 (1992).

Clauson, J. Earl. *These Plantations.* Providence, RI: Roger Williams Press, 1937.

Clemence, Clara Wade. "Ram-Tail Factory." *Windham County Transcript,* 1948.

Coleman, Peter J. *The Transformation of Rhode Island, 1790–1860.* Providence, RI: Brown University Press, 1963.

D'Agostino, Thomas, and Arlene Nicholson. *Abandoned Villages and Ghost Towns of New England.* Atglen, PA: Schiffer Books, 2008.

———. *Haunted Rhode Island.* Atglen, PA: Schiffer Books, 2006.

———. *Legends, Lore and Secrets of New England.* Charleston, SC: The History Press, 2013.

Evans, Oliver. *Young Mill-Wrights and Miller's Guide.* Philadelphia, PA: Lea and Blanchard, 1850.

Federal Writer's Project. *Rhode Island: A Guide to the Smallest State.* Boston: Houghton Mifflin Company, 1937.

Foster, A Bicentennial Celebration. Providence, RI: Union Printing Co. 1981.

Hare, Augustus. *Epitaphs for Country Churchyards.* Oxford, London: John Henry and James Parker, 1856.

Hopkins, Lytle. "The Ramtail Ghost." *Observer Publications,* October 26, 1961.

Johnson, Keith, and Sandra Johnson. *Paranormal Realities III*. Warwick, RI: NEAR Publishing, 2014.

Matthews, Margery. *Peleg's Last Word: The Story of the Foster Woolen Manufactory*. North Scituate, RI: Cardinal Press, 1987.

———. *So I've Been Told*. Foster, RI: Foster Preservation Society, 1985.

Perry, Amos. *The Census for the State of Rhode Island and Providence Plantations*. Providence, RI: E.L. Freeman & Son, 1887.

Providence Journal Bulletin Almanac: Rhode Island Legends. Providence Journal Bulletin, 1997.

Sloane, Eric. *Our Vanishing Landscape*. Mineola, NY: Dover Publications, Inc., 1955.

Smitten, Susan. *Ghost Stories of New England*. Auburn, WA: Lone Pine Publishing, 2003.

St. Pierre, Joseph. "Ghosts at Ramtail?" *Observer Publications*, October 25, 1973.

Wilkinson, Reverend Israel. *Memoirs of the Wilkinson Family in America*. Jacksonville, IL: Davis and Penniman, 1869.

OTHER SOURCES

Book of Deeds, Burrilleville, Rhode Island, various volumes.

Book of Deeds, Foster, Rhode Island, vols. 1–36.

Foster, Rhode Island plat maps.

Foster, Rhode Island Probate Records, vols. 1–5.

Foster, Rhode Island Tax Records, 1870 to 1874.

ABOUT THE AUTHORS

As authors of ten books sold worldwide—*Haunted Rhode Island*; *Haunted New Hampshire*; *Haunted Massachusetts*; *Pirate Ghosts and Phantom Ships*; *Abandoned Villages and Ghost Towns of New England*; *A Guide to Haunted New England*; *A History of Vampires in New England*; *Haunted Vermont*; *Ghost Stories and Legends of Connecticut* and *Legends, Lore and Secrets of New England*—Thomas D'Agostino and Arlene Nicholson have experienced, recorded, photographed and penned the most incredible haunts and legends the region has to offer while becoming among the most prolific and knowledgeable individuals on the subjects of ghosts, legends and folklore.

The Ramtail Factory is just another New England legend that has been a fascination for Tom and Arlene for twenty-two years, from not only the haunted side but the historical, as well.

With thirty-two years of experience and over one thousand investigations, it is no wonder Tom and Arlene have appeared on numerous radio and television shows and documentaries, including A&E Biography Channel's *My Ghost Story*, WGBY's *Things That Go Bump in the Night: Tales of Haunted New England*, the PBS documentary series *Haunted Rhode Island* and Animal Planet's *The Haunted*, as well as several appearances on *Ghosts R Near*, *30 Odd Minutes* and *Ghost Chronicles*, to name a few.

Their paranormal experiences and stories have appeared in countless publications worldwide. Tom and Arlene are the organizers of Paranormal United Research Society. They are well respected and celebrated for their years of experience and knowledge in the fields of New England history and the paranormal.